Upsetting the Table

A Business Fable

Shannon,

Enjoy.

Robbie Hardy

6/7/16

This book is dedicated to all my "sisters" – to my mother, my sister, my daughter, my sisters-in-law, my nieces of all varieties and all of my friends and colleagues who give me inspiration, make me laugh, sometimes make me cry, but who always have my back.

Table of Contents

Acknowledgements

I have had many challenging experiences in my career where I never thought I would be successful. At that those points, it seemed like time stood still, or it rushed by so fast I could hardly breathe. When I took my seat at the table many years ago, I was the only woman. While that remained the case for many years to come, it never stopped me from driving towards whatever goal or result was in front of me. I was fortunate in that I did not accept that being a woman was a problem to be solved, but rather I was there to do a job and do it well. My female colleagues outwardly had the same approach, but perhaps inside all of our heads was this chant, "We have to be better to be equal." We all worked hard to break the "glass ceiling" in our own ways (and together as a movement) and while doing it, it seemed like we made great progress. However, today when the Equal Rights Amendment is still not in the constitution, and women's pay is still at 77% of a man's, it seems we peaked a few years ago. Yet it is never too late to achieve equality between men and women, each of us just has to take our seat at the table and leverage it for the many.

Now I have the luxury of reflecting back on all of those times and turn those rewarding and challenging experiences into this business fable to share. Writing this book was a way to impart the lessons I've earned the hard way over my career. I will tell you that writing this book feels like one of my hardest, but most rewarding achievements.

I had always wanted to do something BIG for mentoring young women that was scalable and reached far more than I could one-on-one. I also always felt like I had a book or two in me, but I had no idea where or how to begin. I was fortunate to be introduced to a book coach, editor, ghostwriter, etc., etc., extraordinaire, Jaqueline Kyle. Jaqueline has written several books of her own and helped many write their own books. She is a bright, driven young woman, who has held my hand, listened to me whine, made me laugh, recorded my experiences, read my blogs and other materials, and turned them all into chapters. Who knew anyone could do such an incredible feat? She humbles me. Together we have created this amazing first book on mentoring women. Readers will be able to get a taste of what mentorship is all about and hopefully it will inspire women to greater success.

My daughter, Tonya Dale, another incredibly talented woman, created the cover for this book... she is extraordinary in everything she does and she means the world to me. I love you, Tonya, and I am so proud of you, and of course, this awesome cover.

I had a team of naming consultants who worked tirelessly to help me name this book, at some point the creation of the book seemed easier than the name! My naming team was my awesome friend Ann Miller, her creative husband Charlie (I call him Mr. Miller), and my rock, my very best friend, and my husband, Robert Dale. They put up with whiteboards and flip charts and endless emails until <u>Upsetting the Table</u> was born. I cannot thank them enough for all their ideas, their incredible

sense of humor and their tolerance for my wanting just a little bit more.

My biggest thanks goes to my husband, because in addition to being on the naming team, he also had to "deal with me" while I went on this roller coaster book-writing ride. He is the love of my life, my best friend, and just an overall kind and great man who thankfully loves strong women.

Introduction

What you are holding, right now in your hands, is a career's worth of knowledge. You can read it, drop it, use it as coaster, or a doorstop; the knowledge inside this book is for you to use as you please. It isn't fragile; in fact, it is pretty universal and once you see the knowledge for what it is, you will see it being applied every day, in every aspect of day-to-day life. You can apply it in your life too.

This is your guide to success in the workplace. Only, it isn't a boring How-To book. Or, the latest self-help, stand-on-your-head-and-chant book. It actually is a story about a young woman facing her first major project in a middle-management role. Through her eyes we'll explore the challenges of the workplace, navigating politics, sexism, and a crippling lack of self-esteem. Helping her through these challenges is Liz, her mentor and a basic stand in for me, Robbie Hardy, the author.

I had my first great experience being a mentor in the 1980s. It was amazing to see how the career of this first young lady grew and blossomed with just the tiniest bit of guidance. That one interaction launched a passion for mentorship that has lasted my entire career. In 1995, after selling my first software company, I actually created a shell for a fund to focus on bolstering young women's self-esteem. But, many years and many mentorees passed. I still could not see how to "bottle" the secret sauce of one-on-one and one-to-many sessions.

It wasn't until my career began to wind down that I finally had the space to re-engage with this large-scale mentorship dream. By that time, I had amassed a wealth of knowledge on start-ups, mentoring, and an outrage for the systematic marginalization of women in the workplace. The time was ripe for a change in the boardroom. For upsetting the table.

Are you ready to Upset the Table?

This book is a taste of what mentorship is all about. It illustrates what mentorship relationships should look like and how they can be used to benefit a career. It's told as a business fable for a reason. Sometimes it is easier to see how a friend confronts their problems than to spot the problems in our own lives. By following along on this journey, hopefully you can get comfortable with some uncomfortable truths, face up to some career debilitating behaviors, and leverage this knowledge into something you can take action with in your own life.

If you are a woman and find the knowledge here valuable, I would encourage you to seek out a mentor for your career. There are many seasoned women willing to teach and guide as I have and as Liz does in the book. In fact, there is a new mentorship organization called Lessons Earned that pairs mentors with mentorees. You'll learn more about Lessons Earned throughout the course of this book.

I am so excited to finally be sharing some of the many lessons I have earned. This business fable is a culmination of years of experience, reflection, and passion for women taking their seat at the table. I hope you can use some of the practical advice in your own life. As you read, keep track of your thoughts and *ah-ha!* moments with the *Taking My Seat* daily journal. Go to the Lessons Earned website or Amazon to get your journal. And please, sign up for a mentor or to be a mentor!

– Robbie Hardy

Chapter 1

Jessica

"Come on, Jessica! Let's find seats in front."

Jessica thought she should have known better. All morning Sarah had been chiding Jessica and chivvying her along to a professional development conference that Jessica hadn't actually agreed to go to in good faith. She had planned to declare some sort of personal tragedy and sit in front of the TV after Sarah went on without her... As Jessica's roommate, Sarah knew her too well and headed her off at every pass, going so far as to get her suit dry cleaned and presenting it to her with a coffee first thing in the morning.

Now Jessica gave up all hope of sitting in the back of the hall and sneaking out early as Sarah commandeered her arm and steered her towards the empty seats by the stage.

"This is perfect," Sarah smiled, placing her folder and notebook on the front row, center seat.

"This had better not be like school, or a comedy show, where they choose people in the front row," Jessica warned.

"I have no idea," Sarah grinned and handed the day's schedule to Jessica with a wink.

Jessica settled into her chair to study the one-day event, with four speakers, broken up with breaks and a lunch. The whole thing wrapped up with an evening mixer for networking. *Ugh. Networking.*

"Do we have to stay for-" Jessica looked up and realized that Sarah had dropped her note-taking materials and immediately wandered off to chat with a small clump of people in business suits. She seemed to be the center of attention and beaming.

Jessica watched her with a mix of jealousy and awe. Sarah was so confident and natural talking with strangers. When Jessica tried something like that she was too shy to open her mouth and often stood unnoticed on the periphery of the group, wishing fervently to be anywhere else.

To pass the time until the program started (Sarah insisted that they get there 20 minutes early), Jessica read through the bios of each of the speakers. One caught her eye. It was for Liz Schaffer. Her bio declared, *Serial entrepreneur and passionate wine drinker, Liz believes firmly that experience is the best teacher. In her groundbreaking career, Liz helped launch three multimillion-dollar technology companies, managed to raise capital for countless technology start-ups and has developed and then sold five small businesses in her spare time. She is a passionate mentor of young women and an advocate for women's rights. She recently turned down a teaching position at Harvard business school, citing the fact that she didn't have a college education. Liz didn't invent bootstrapping, but she perfected the art of building a company from nothing.*

Jessica's heart beat a little faster as she contemplated what all of those experiences might feel like. By her picture, Liz looked to be in her late 50s, with blonde hair fading into silver and small wrinkles by her eyes that emphasized her enthusiastic smile. Jessica suspected Liz might not live up to her hype and consulted the program to find Liz slated last, before the program wrapped up for networking.

The lights dimmed briefly twice, and the chatter died down. Soon enough, Sarah found her way back to their seats. Jessica showed Sarah the bios and pointed out how different Liz seemed.

Sarah grinned with a twinkle in her eye, "I guess you'll have to stick it out *all day* to find out."

Jessica and Sarah stood stretching in the break between speakers.

"What do you think?"

Jessica bit her lower lip. "The networking talk seemed interesting, I guess." In truth, the speaker on networking had made her feel paranoid and self-conscious. She had never thought about her "elevator speech" before, but it couldn't have been that bad. Now, she would feel rehearsed and stilted if an "elevator opportunity" ever came up – which it certainly would at the networking meeting tonight. Jessica had underlined _Prepare to talk for ten floors – NOT a 100 story building!_ in her notes. Next to it she had doodled an elevator in free-fall, complete with doomed stick figures.

Sarah waved a dismissive hand. "That's old hat." To emphasize her point, Sarah eyed the room, trying to spot someone to talk with. It had been the same at lunch and during the morning break as well. Jessica had concluded that maybe Sarah had insisted she come to save her seat and babysit her purse. She had said as much after lunch and Sarah had contritely agreed to spend more time with her. Sarah was so extroverted it was sometimes tough to be with her.

Sarah paused her scan, finding her mark. "Do you see that guy over there?" Sarah nodded to a group of men in the center aisle.

"Uh, yeah." Jessica agreed, figuring it didn't matter exactly which one she was referring to.

"He was telling me this morning that he had been to this thing before. He said the speakers always change, but the format doesn't. The best speaker is always last."

"Liz?"

"I guess," Sarah shrugged.

The lights dimmed, and Jessica immediately settled back into her seat. She flipped her notebook to a fresh page and clicked her pen open.

When Liz took the stage, Jessica noted that she looked just like her picture, smiling and warm, but there was something in her posture, the way that she held herself that hinted at the steel spine beneath her friendly exterior. She thanked the crowd and launched into her talk on body language and communication in the workplace.

"Did you know," Liz started, "that when you are talking, giving a presentation, or trying to impress a date, that what you *say* only makes up part of the message the other person receives?

"Who here has ever said something sarcastic? Did the person know it was sarcastic from the words? Or the way that you said it? The way that you say something is called tone. Tone is how you turn a 'you look great!' genuine compliment into 'you look *great*." Liz dragged out the *great* to sound as if there were 15 a's in the word. There were a few chuckles in the crowd.

"Charming, isn't it?" Liz laughed. "But that's not the end of the communication tango our minds interpret to figure out the message. No! We also have *body language.* This is particularly fun because whether you realize it or not, your whole body is talking. All the time."

Liz bounced up onto her toes and pitched up her voice. "You look great!" She dropped a shoulder and cocked her head. "You look *great.*" The audience laughed a bit more enthusiastically this time. The petite silver-haired woman had just nailed the creepy, street side, cat-caller.

"That's a bit disturbing," she acknowledged, starting to pace and work the stage like a performer at a comedy club. A slide appeared with a pie chart behind the pacing Liz.

"Research shows that 7% of communication comes from what you say. The words that come out of your mouth. Another 38% of communication comes from tone. Body language counts for a whopping 55% of how your message is received."

She stopped center stage and the screen went blank. "Now, how do we communicate today?" She mimed typing. She mimed texting. She held an imaginary phone out to the audience to see. "How much tone and body language can you get from this?"

Behind her the screen lit up with a popular sketch from Key and Peele. The ensuing text message confusion led to one side jumping up and down screaming and the other person saying, "Aw, isn't he great?" It escalated to the two meeting where one friend wants to treat another to a drink, and the other entering the bar with a barbed baseball bat.

The crowd roared with laughter and recognition.

Liz reappeared at the end of the clip and raised a hand. "Who here has had something similar happen?"

Jessica raised her hand and sensed the entire room had raised theirs too.

"Keep your hand raised if this has happened in the workplace."

Jessica lowered her hand unobtrusively. In truth, there had been many mis-communications at the office, and she had only been there three months. But, she didn't want anyone to know that. Jessica glanced to her side to see if Sarah had noticed, but saw Sarah still had her hand raised and was staring raptly at the stage.

"I can see a few of you squirming out there," Liz said wryly. "Thanks for your honesty, but I'm not going to call on anyone to share."

She started her pacing again, lecturing, questioning, holding the audience's attention. "Work-place miscommunication can be fatal. Not to you literally, but your career? Yes. Your business? Yes. Let's take a look at that chart again." The pie chart slide flickered back on screen.

"Seven percent! Only 7% of what you mean actually comes through in communication. The best advice I can possibly give you, is that if you have a difficult message to deliver, get out of your chair and go over to talk to the person. If they aren't in your office, pick up the phone. Get yourself that added 38% of tone to help get your message across.

"And never. Ever. Send a message in anger. You know what I mean!" She paused her pacing and started pantomiming typing, punching each imaginary key with extra emphasis... "Because for some reason, that email is read EXACTLY as you meant it." The audience laughed. "Anger is a universal language. People seem to easily recognize anger. But they are slower to hear compassion and understanding."

She resumed striding up and down the stage. "Pick up the phone. Get out of the chair. Talk on Skype. Whatever you have to do to get face to face, eyeball to eyeball."

Jessica thought that might be the best advice she had heard all day. It would have certainly have saved her an uncomfortable encounter and the resulting meeting in her boss's office that felt a bit like being sent to the principal.

The pie chart dissolved into an image of an office, with chairs, a bookshelf and a plant in the corner. "Let's talk about ways we can use body language to move our careers and ourselves to the next level."

On screen, a person appeared in the office. He is relaxed and smiling, his shoulders are back, standing straight and his hand is out as if to greet someone. Liz proceeded to point these things out, and arrows appeared around the man to point out each positive attribute.

Next a woman appeared. Her face is neutral, but since the guy is smiling at her, she looks a bit stern and shut off. Her notebook was clutched to her chest and her shoulders were rotated slightly forward, giving the impression that she was hunching protectively over the contents inside. Jessica blinked in surprise. Add a coffee mug and glasses and she might have been staring at a caricature of herself. It hurt to look at it.

The arrows appeared next and Jessica watched the character correct her body language one item at a time. *If only it were that easy.*

Liz ran through a number of scenarios. The man stood too close to the woman and crushed her hand when shaking it. The woman fidgeted and didn't make eye contact. The solutions were presented with more pointing arrows.

A conference room appeared on the screen next. It featured a long table in the center of the room with chairs around it. The periphery walls were also crowded with chairs.

"Whose office has a conference room like this?" Again Jessica raised her hand and felt most of the audience raise theirs behind her.

"Silly, isn't it?" Liz asked and the crowd chuckled back. "There are whole theories about board rooms and the politics of meetings. Do you come early? Do you come late? Do you make an entrance? Are you already seated? Where do you sit? All that stuff that goes on, believe it or not. People are obsessed with these sorts of power plays – or what they perceive to be power plays."

"What's absurd about all of it is that the actual results you get stem from your body language. Not when you arrive or where your actual seat is at the table." She paused and seemed to consider what she would say next. "If you are not sure when to enter a room, it shows." The screen populated with people sitting at the table and a guy standing hesitantly in the doorway.

"If you take confidence from reading an article that says, 'be early' or 'be late' or 'stand on your head' then when you come into the room and do exactly what you read, your body language matches that confidence. People respond to confidence. So people respond and respect you."

The room cleared of people and this time the woman appeared. Jessica noticed her back was straight this time and her notebook was no longer hugged protectively to her chest. She was sitting in a chair against the wall.

"It doesn't matter where you sit at the table," Liz intoned. "What's wrong with this picture?"

After a pause someone shouted from the back of the room, "She's not AT the table!"

Jessica's eyes flew back to the screen. The voice was right. The woman was sitting with her back to the wall in an empty room. All the chairs at the conference table were open, she had chosen to sit with her back against the wall, away from the table.

"Yes. This comes from insecurity, or being polite. Or maybe a lack of self-esteem. The problem with this picture is that once the meeting starts, the people sitting at the walls are instantly spectators, not participants."

The chairs populated with people, the ones sitting by the walls are straining to see over the shoulders of the people at the table. "They aren't even *good* spectator seats, folks."

Liz regarded the crowd. "I know that some of you recognize yourself in this. It's okay. The great thing about these meetings is that there are usually two or three a week. You will have a chance to fix this impression. Here's how you do it."

Bullet points appeared over the scene, appearing individually as Liz talked through each technique.

"Take a breath," Liz read. "Practice outside the room if you need to, in the ladies' room, in your cubicle or office. But when you walk in, you need to project confidence, even if you don't feel it inside. You have to make that first good impression for the rest of this to work."

"So, you step into the room. You say hello to the people already there. You stick your hand out; you make eye contact. Can you see yourself doing these things? Good. Now put your notepad and pen in front of a chair."

Jessica took notes. Her heart was racing and her breathing was shallow. She felt like she was about to be let in on a mysterious secret that everyone else seemed to be born knowing and she had somehow missed.

"Take a seat at the table." Liz paused. "Your heart may be racing, but no one is going to relegate you to the side of the room... You will be amazed how quickly you will go from being a spectator to being a member of the team, whether you deserve it or not.

"'Ah,' I can hear you think," Liz objected to herself. "'What if the table is already full?' That's when you ask the people at the table to make room." She paused and let the audience consider. Then she slowly pantomimed pulling a chair up to an imaginary table and asked the imaginary inhabitants to "squeeze in." Apparently her imaginary friends didn't move far enough or fast enough. Soon she was wiggling her chair, throwing elbows and squeezing her way to the table. The audience laughed in appreciation.

"People will move for you. They always do. Someone might not want you at the table, but they won't object. They don't know if you just got a promotion, a new assignment, or something significant to contribute that you didn't have before. They won't kick you out because they don't know who they could offend in the process."

Jessica tried to imagine herself in that scenario and smiled. Yes. This was possible. She could do this. Maybe not the absurd elbowing and wiggling in, but show up early and claim a spot? Yes, she thought she could manage that.

"You are an employee of the company. If you're not, you still have a reason to be there. You should be there." Liz emphasized. "You are part of the team. Take your place at the table."

Jessica felt a weight come off her chest and she exhaled slowly. She nodded to herself. Yes, she could do this.

A stone tablet engraved with a coffee cup appeared on the screen. "One last thing before we wrap up here, folks." Liz paused dramatically. "It is the 11th commandment of the work place. Unless your job title is 'personal assistant,' *thou shalt not fetch anyone else's coffee, tea, water, soda, or beverage of choice*." The crowd roared with approval. "It's common courtesy to ask if you're already up. But, you are no one's parent in the office. Don't get too hung up on being anyone's slave. It cannot happen unless you allow it. When a meeting is happening and someone looks for coffee, tell them where the break room is and hold your seat."

The crowd applauded when Liz took her bow. Jessica turned to Sarah with a smile. "That was really good!"

"Yes, it was," Sarah agreed. "Maybe we can meet her during the networking."

Jessica's heart dropped. She had forgotten about the networking.

Note From Robbie:

I cannot emphasize enough, the importance of stretching yourself and taking on things that are not very comfortable when you contemplate them... These stretches are necessary to grow and expand your knowledge and your mind.

The more you open yourself up to new learning opportunities and new chances, the greater your capacity to shore up your foundation, gain introspection, and grow as a person, parent, professional, or partner. This stretching also opens up your ability to listen and actually hear new ideas, new ways of thinking, and incorporate them into your life...

Personal development conferences, coaches, and continuing education programs all contribute to your inner well-being. The more you open yourself up to learning opportunities, the greater your capacity to shore up your foundation, gain introspection, and grow as a person, parent, professional or partner.

Chapter 2

Liz

Networking was exhausting in a way that speaking was not.

Liz had left the stage riding a wave of applause. She had intended to surf the swell of enthusiasm as long as she could, until she washed up on the shore of reality, littered with the mundane debris of emails, text messages, and grocery lists. As in any good performance, she had given the crowd her energy and they had returned it in earnest, leaving her elated.

She had been the star speaker of the program, and had been highly sought after in the networking hour. She had smiled, shook hands, and exchanged cards with over a 100 people. The room was filled with shifting, chatting, card-wielding business suits. As the tides of people circled about the room, breaking and regrouping, Liz slipped away to discreetly stretch her feet. The high heels were so comfortable in the store and now would be relegated to the rack marked, "to be worn when only standing for less than 30 minutes!"

"Um. Hi."

Liz glanced up and saw a young woman with glasses in a neatly cut business suit, smiling shyly with her hand out... Liz smiled and took the proffered hand.

"I really liked your presentation."

"Thank you," Liz waited for her to say something else but the young woman seemed to be at a loss for words. Liz asked, "What did you like about the presentation?" before the silence could get too awkward.

To her surprise, the woman's eyes teared up and she quietly said, "I am one of the spectators. I sit on the side of the room." She cleared her throat and forced herself to go on a little stronger. "I always sit with my back against the wall trying be invisible. I went to Berkeley, I had a 3.9 GPA, but I am so shy it hurts!"

"Oh, you are not alone, my dear!" Liz straightened. "Do you feel like you can take your seat at the table now?"

The girl drew a deep breath and let it out slowly,

shrugging and trying to shake something off her shoulders as she did. She raised her head and met Liz's eyes. She smiled a little at the corners of her mouth and gave a nod. Liz thought, *This is why I give this talk! I sure hope that confidence is still there in the morning.*

"Do me a big favor. At your next meeting sit at the table. Get there early; it is easier and go for it... Liz pulled out her card and handed it to the young woman. "Tell me how it goes."

The girl's eyes went wide and a true smile broke onto her face. "Okay." She took the card and turned to leave.

"Wait," Liz called. "What's your name?"

"Jessica."

Note From Robbie:

Finding a mentor can be a bit of a challenge. Where do you look? How do you know they are right for you? There are mentors all around you if you get out of your comfort zone and ask! Talk, ask questions, and gather information about how other people have found mentors! You do not need to reinvent the wheel; take the time to learn *about* the wheel.

A good mentor is generous with their time and is willing to meet you on your level. That means, that when you meet with you mentor, your mentor is focused on **you**, not telling his or her own war stories. A great mentor realizes they have already accomplished and played the game in the big leagues and that you need help to get on the field (or in the stadium).

Often times people get caught up in their egos. They need for everyone around them to acknowledge them. They say things like, "I closed this deal. I am friends with so-and-so, I am so important because..." A good mentor realizes that it is not about "them" and their accomplishments. It's about taking the time to understand where the mentoree is and what they need to move towards their personal definition of success.

In the situation we just saw, Liz could have easily blown Jessica off. However, Liz realized that she had already made an impact on Jessica and that Jessica was willing to learn and try new things. She met her on that level to encourage Jessica to take that first step towards her seat at the table.

Chapter 3
Asking For Help

Jessica had walked by the conference room and glanced in before turning the corner and taking temporary refuge by the copy machine. She scanned a document and pressed "Copy" letting the machine buy her time. No one had been in the room yet, but the meeting was not supposed to start for another five minutes. As the machine hummed and chugged and spit out copies, Jessica rolled her shoulders back, taking a deep breath. She straightened her head and tried to visualize walking into the room, bypassing the chairs by the wall, and taking a seat at the conference table. *It's not impolite. There is room at the table for me.*

Jessica became aware of a small cough behind her and turned with a start to find an intern from the marketing department waiting for the copy machine. She hastily scooped the copies from the machine and headed to the conference room.

Standing inside and chatting were two men she recognized but had never spoken to.

Jessica fought every instinct to slide into the room unnoticed. She closed her eyes briefly and conjured up the image of the confident caricature from the presentation before walking into the room.

Her shoulder blades felt a little odd, being drawn away from her ears, but it reminded her to keep her head up. She surprised herself a little by meeting one of the men's eyes and giving a friendly smile before passing him, placing her copies in front of a chair at the table and taking the seat. Her heart hammered and she bit her lips to keep herself from grinning. *This is no big deal!*

For the next few minutes, the meeting participants filtered through the doors in singles and pairs. Jessica held her posture and no one batted an eye at her. When the table filled to capacity, she held her ground and didn't allow herself to feel obligated to give up her seat. *First come, first serve. Early bird gets the worm. I'm part of this team too!* she silently told each latecomer.

As in many companies, her team leader and boss, Ken, came into the room five minutes after the specified meeting time. It seemed rude, but part of the company culture. Those present were on time and anyone coming through the door from now on was late. Jessica passed out the agendas she had copied before coming into the room. When Ken asked who would take notes for this meeting, Jessica refused to volunteer and someone on the side of the room filled the void.

Jessica found it hard to pay attention to the meeting. Her eyes would wander to individual faces, linger on the speakerphone in the center of the table, marveling at her new-found confidence and where it had landed her. Unfortunately, being at the table had also made her more visible to everyone else, and Ken in particular.

"How about you, Jessica?" Ken asked.

Every eye swiveled toward her. Without notes to take she had let her mind wander and she realized with horror that she had no idea what the topic was. Jessica prayed it was a yes or no question.

"Um. Yes."

"Good. Two weeks should be enough time," Ken surmised and ticked something off on his notepad. The meeting proceeded, Jessica now paying keen attention to the proceedings, hoping to glean some idea of what she had just agreed to. The meeting broke up without yielding further clues, and Jessica had to scramble to find the note taker and get an early copy.

Liz answered the phone on the second ring. Normally she would have let the call ring to voicemail, she was vehement about time blocking and respecting her own work time... But today her desk was covered in things that she really did not want to do and she was trying very hard to muster the discipline to keep going. A local call was a bit too tempting.

"Hello?"

"Hi," the voice hesitated, confused... "May I speak with Liz Schaffer, please?"

"Speaking," Liz smiled. People were always shocked that she answered her own phone and she had never understood why. She was not one to stand on ceremony, she was either available to talk to she was not, voicemail took care of the rest.

"My name is Jessica Wexler... We met at the professional development conference last week? You gave me your card to tell you how my first attempt to sit at the table went." There was a pause on the line and then she clarified, "I've always been a spectator, not a participant."

Liz racked her brain to place a face with this voice and suddenly the young woman with the glasses was there. The shy one. "Yes! Jessica, how are you? How did it go?"

"I think I screwed up!" she blurted.

"Oh dear. What happened?"

"I was at the table!" Jessica exclaimed. She tried to catch control of herself and failed, letting the words stream out of her mouth in one great big gush. "I was at the table for the meeting. I didn't take notes, I didn't get coffee, I didn't give up my chair when the room was full. I had my shoulders back and my head high. I even met a team member's eye! And I was so excited to be there I stopped paying attention and now," her voice sped up even more, "I'm-in-charge-of-a-project-and-I'm-not-sure-I-know-how-to-do-it!"

Liz could hear Jessica trying to catch her breath on the other side of the line. Liz's heart soared on behalf of the young woman – her first major project! She bit back a smile and let herself slip into coaching mode.

"Alright Jessica, let's talk this through." Liz took the silence as assent and continued, "Why did you want to sit at the table?"

Jessica's answer came fast, without thought. "To be taken seriously."

"Right. And you took your seat at the table and what happened?"

"They took me seriously."

"Exactly."

There was a silence as Jessica worked on her next thought. Liz found herself interested in where this conversation was going. The evolution of Jessica

Wexler, shy networker to Jessica Wexler, nervous project leader intrigued her.

"I didn't expect that it would work so well. So fast I mean," she corrected herself. "I don't know if I can do this."

Liz smiled, connecting with that feeling that happened before she launched every new business, the feeling before every deal, even before every speech. Yes, she could relate.

"You *can* do this. I don't know what you do for a living, but I know that you are smart and capable. You took the initiative to come to the conference, to learn. You can learn and master whatever this is too."

"My roommate dragged me to that conference. The only reason I didn't leave before the networking is because she drove," Jessica confessed.

Liz tried not to laugh. This poor girl did not give herself any credit. "Do you want to succeed?"

"Yes." Again, her answer was firm and fast.

Liz ran through all the possible scenarios of help she could offer. The attagirl hadn't worked. She had a speech about this hidden somewhere in the depths of her computer, but somehow she didn't think sending Jessica the slides would make the difference. And, Liz realized that she *did* want to roll up her sleeves and make a difference for Jessica.

"Meet me tomorrow," Liz ordered, "for coffee before work. I'm going to help you to envision your success."

"Are you sure you have the ti–"

"Yes." Liz quickly arranged the details and hung up. The tasks on her desk were still here, still boring, but she did each one imagining what it would be like to confront them as a novice. By the end of the day her mind was full of thoughts and advice for Jessica.

Note From Robbie:

Let's take moment here to define *mentorship*. According to Wikipedia, **Mentorship** *is a relationship in which a more experienced or more knowledgeable person helps to guide a less experienced or less knowledgeable person. The mentor may be older or younger, but have a certain area of expertise.*

So, why would two people begin a mentorship relationship? Well, in Jessica's case it seems obvious. She is taking on a new challenge in her life and is looking for guidance, support, and expertise that she is not getting anywhere else. The trickier side is Liz, and all the similar "Liz's" in the real world.

I have mentored over 40 women over the course of my professional career. These relationships were unpaid, unofficial, and incredibly rewarding. It's funny how much you learn about yourself and your experiences when you're seeing similar stories play out for someone else...

One of the biggest rewards of being a mentor is watching people grow into places and things they never even conceived of in the beginning. Often the biggest success is helping someone define what personal success means for them – not how others do it and then trying to emulate it. It's amazing to watch the self-confidence and self-esteem build, often exponentially. Success is such an individual thing and helping people see that and then grab it and go for it, is incredible.

Chapter 4

Mentorship

Jessica arrived at the coffee shop 20 minutes early to order a latte and grab a place for her and Liz to sit. She placed her folio, straining with meeting notes and research she had been able to glean from the company computer system, on the table. It was daunting to look at all this information and her eyes would zone out if she stared at it too long.

It hadn't been easy to call Liz. She had picked up the phone because it was the closest thing to ripping off a Band-Aid. If she had emailed and received no response, she would have read and re-read her email inquiry obsessively, trying to divine what she had said wrong that led Liz to pass her over. By calling she would be sent to voicemail or a personal assistant. The result would be the same, but then she would have no digital trace to obsess over afterwards. It was an utter shock when Liz had answered her phone and flabbergasting that she was about to meet her for coffee.

Liz dropped into the chair opposite of Jessica, startling her. "If I had seen you come in, I would have bought your coffee." Jessica glanced about, trying to figure out where Liz had materialized from. A cup of coffee steamed in her hand. Liz noticed her confusion and pointed toward the barista. "They know my order and when I come in. They leave a café au lait on the counter at 6:55 and I leave them whatever cash is in my purse. It works out well for both of us."

Jessica met Liz's eyes. They sparked with barely contained laughter. Jessica grinned.

"Thank you for doing this," Jessica said, still not sure what 'this' was, but incredibly grateful that she wasn't alone.

"I see a very thick stack of papers there."

Jessica glanced down and suddenly saw it from Liz's point of view. "Oh no! I don't expect you to go through it with me. I just... can't let it out of my sight."

Liz nodded, as if that made any sort of sense, then picked up the folio and placed it under the table, hiding it. "Better?"

Jessica thought for a moment and nodded, "Yeah."

"I thought about you a lot last night... I was remembering all the times I have been new and scared or sometimes not new but still scared..." Liz held her hand up to forestall Jessica's objection. "There's no shame in being scared; in fact, it helps keep you honest and fresh. No judgment. If we are going to do this, let's be honest with each other, okay?"

"What is this?" Jessica asked warily.

"Coaching, advising, mentoring, whatever you want to call it. With your permission, I'm going to help you find your own success."

Jessica was gob-smacked. She eyed the table trying to work her thoughts out. "You want to help me. Succeed. At what?"

"Whatever success means to you," Liz smiled...

Jessica smiled uncertainly. "I'm sorry if this is rude, but why? What's in it for you?" *Do I need to pay you?* she wondered.

"It's a good question. The short answer is, I like to coach and mentor. As far as tangibles go, no, I don't expect you to pay me. I expect you will lean on me to ask questions, bounce ideas off of, and essentially get out of your own head. In return, I learn just as much from you as you do from me."

Jessica must have looked incredulous because Liz laughed and continued, "Trust me, it always works out that way. I learn so much from everyone I work with and I really enjoy it. I wish there had been a coach or mentor in my early days, but I was the only woman in the room or at the table." Liz smiled. "The bottom line is, there is plenty in this for both of us. If you are game, I am game."

Jessica nodded. She was surprised that Liz could think she would learn anything from her but she was game... If Liz was for real, this would be career changing.

Liz smiled broadly. "I know you saw me speak, but what you might not realize is that my career started kind of by accident. I am not good on detail, but I understand concepts. I ended up in the software business, on the management side. I wasn't a programmer, I got through the first few hurdles just by acting like I knew what I was doing, but not really knowing at all.

"Every day I would feel overwhelmed. Inadequate. I was scared that people would find out and I would lose my job. I needed to work to put my husband – now ex – through graduate school. People would use these abbreviations and acronyms and I would just, hold my breath." Liz passed a hand over her face, and tilted her head. Jessica could totally relate.

"I got through it by pausing, taking a deep breath, and saying, 'okay, here I am, I can do this.' In the beginning I listened, I agreed to all sorts of things, and then figured out what they were and how to deliver it later.

"Now this," Liz gestured to the papers under the table, "tells me that you can do the same thing. You said 'yes,' you took on a project outside of your knowledge sphere, and you're not backing away from it. This is huge! You are taking it on full-force and you're willing to seek help to get it done. Take a moment to just recognize that and give yourself credit for that."

Jessica tried to examine herself from Liz's point of view. She nodded slowly in agreement. "Thank you."

"Trust me... It's hard to find people who will actually take initiative. Most people wait to be told what to do, when to do it, how to do it, and then they want to know what's in it for them when it's all over... Having initiative is a great quality to work with, and it will serve you well. You will grow faster and rise farther than your peers if you are always pushing the edge of your boundaries."

Jessica listened raptly for the next 20 minutes as Liz took turns pumping her up, giving her practical advice, and guiding her on what to do next. She left the coffee shop feeling like a weight had been lifted from her chest.

Note From Robbie:

It's important to set ground rules in a mentoring relationship. It draws lines and expectations for the scope of the relationship and can help curtail uncomfortable situations before they happen. For example, some people are only comfortable with work topics and react badly to advice in a personal sphere.

While each mentorship relationship is different, here are some of my tried and true guidelines:

Trust and Respect at All Times: Trust, that both parties are looking for the best possible outcome. Respect, in particular, that the relationship is voluntary and should not be abused.

Mentorship is a Marathon; Not a Sprint: Results don't happen overnight. Have patience.

Mentors are NOT Parents: Mentors aren't meant to call you every morning and ask if you are ready for work. Ideally, the mentorship relationship is led by the current needs of the mentoree, reaching out for the support they need, when they need it.

Mentors Do NOT take a Role in the Mentoree's Business or Company: Entering into a financial arrangement undermines the mentor relationship... Any advice could no longer be characterized as "in the best interest of the mentoree," if the mentor stands to make a financial gain from the actions they take...

Have a Sense of Humor and Compassion: A mentor has to have a sense of humor and compassion. You have to be able to laugh.

Leave Your Ego at the Door: No one should go out of their way to impress anyone else. Ego-stroking and face-saving only create obstacles to solutions.

Chapter 5

Giving Back

The morning coffee with Jessica had jumpstarted Liz's day. She felt energetic and optimistic after the meeting and had carried that into the rest of her day. Now she sat, speech completed, at a luncheon in a downtown hotel. Attendance for the event was at capacity and the walls of the meeting room had been removed to create space for the tables and the crowd... The food was surprisingly good and Liz munched on it while watching the second presentation. There would be three. She was not the keynote on this occasion, but instead had gone first, to warm up the crowd as the salads were served.

Liz had been a last minute addition; the scheduled speaker was stuck in Chicago in a terrible storm that had closed the airport. Her good friend Nancy, a member of the board for this event, had called in a panic at eight the previous night. Liz agreed, of course, but she wished she had had a little more prep time to look at the conference agenda and tailor her message a bit more for the crowd. The assembled group was a broad demographic; baby boomers, retirees, and some hopeful millennials and as a result, her topic, *visioning*, had been kind of flat. She thought the content was not what they were looking for, but from experience she knew her speech had resonated with someone; it always did.

The overall conference was about literacy. It had been a bit of a shock to learn that the illiteracy they were discussing was here, in the US, her state, her county. Until today, she assumed illiteracy was something people struggled with in third world countries in very rural areas, where children were forced to leave school early and help in the fields.

The speakers were educating her, that's for sure. Early in the talk, Liz pulled out her notepad and started taking notes and recorded the speakers contact information so she could learn more one on one. The slide currently being discussed displayed these alarming statistics:

- 50% of adults cannot read a book written at an eighth grade level
- 45 million are functionally illiterate and read below a 5th grade level
- 44% of American adults do not read a book in a year
- 6 out of 10 households do not buy a single book in a year

It was stomach churning. Utterly sickening. Thirty years ago Liz had dropped out of college without completing her degree. Over the years she had tried to cope for this "inadequacy" by auditing classes, carefully crafting her resume to cover the missing section, and changing the subject when college came up in small talk. After she became a guest lecturer for several business schools, it never made sense to go back to get her degree. Her experience was her education. But it wasn't until she had to turndown (for the umpteenth time) a board spot for a publicly traded company that she had thrown her hands in the air and embraced her "defect."

It had taken herculean willpower to publicize her lack of degree in her bio. She had done it to make peace with that little voice in her head that claimed she wasn't good enough. It was a funny bio, tongue in cheek, designed to inspire, but really, it was advertising her "warts" to the world.

Now, Liz looked at the literacy statistics with horror and shame. Compared to not being able to read? Her sheepskin hang-ups seemed downright trivial. The current slide detailed coping mechanisms of the illiterate.

- Pretending the lights are too dim in a restaurant to read the menu.

- Not leaving the neighborhood for fear of getting lost without signs.

- Working manual labor because you have no mind-skills to market.

The world must be a terribly frightening and claustrophobic place for the illiterate.

The speech was wrapping up and Liz's mind was whirling. *This needed to be fixed!* She heard her usual entrepreneurial refrain, "There has to be a better way!" Oh how many times had she said those words and then embarked on a journey to find a better way. Perhaps she could volunteer to tutor. Or join a committee. Maybe what this illiteracy thing needed was a national platform. What would it take to create a non-profit? Liz drew a circle around the question, determined to find out.

Note From Robbie:

Paying it Forward: three words that are essential to feel successful and fulfilled. There are astounding benefits that come from volunteer work. Volunteering can lift your spirits, let you see a direct difference you can make in the world, and connect you with people you otherwise would have never met. It can reenergize you when you feel depleted and give you purpose when you feel discouraged.

Most cities and counties strive to provide basic support services to the at-risk and needy in the community. Some are more successful than others, but almost all programs benefit from volunteers. Your community would embrace your contribution to a project or program where you can share your knowledge and experience.

This book discusses the needs of literacy specifically, and Lessons Earned has taken on literacy as its social crusade. We encourage all of our membership to reach out to their local library and volunteer to tutor an adult. Whether you choose to volunteer with this issue or some other, Lessons Earned highly encourages Paying it Forward– for the benefit of all.

Chapter 6
Women Can't Quit

Jessica nervously shuffled the notes in front of her. With Liz's encouragement, Jessica had made an appointment with Ken to review her project progress thus far and discuss the next steps forward. The meeting had been incredibly productive and Jessica had left it feeling good. Now in the team meeting, she was nervous again. Even though it had been a few weeks, it still felt weird to sit at the conference room table when other people sat to the side and peered in. Soon they would be peering directly at her.

Jessica took comfort that the faces at the table were becoming more familiar, more friendly. Alan sat directly to her left. He was young, classically handsome, and unwaveringly confident in himself. He had asked her to lunch a week ago, and with a boost from Liz, she had accepted. Alan was all business and she didn't sense any streak of meanness when he met her eyes and smiled.

Directly across the table was Charlene, who had taken her aside to straighten her necklace a few days ago. Charlene seemed effortlessly flawless. From her unblemished skin to her immaculately shaped nails, it was unnerving how perfectly she turned up to work day in and day out. Jessica smiled nervously at her and Charlene smiled widely in return. Jessica took that for encouragement...

Just taking his seat at the head of the table, was Ken, her boss. He had been impatient when she had asked for their one-on-one meeting, but once they had finally connected he had seemed impressed by how far she had come with the project on her own. He had helped her dissect the stack of research she had unearthed and strategized how she should move forward. He smiled at her now, almost paternally, and she shoved down an uneasy feeling in her gut.

The meeting went around the table, with each member updating the status of their respective projects. When Jessica's turn came, she read directly from her notes, which were creased and somewhat damp from her nervous shuffling. When she finished, she glanced at Ken and he smiled again in that paternal way.

"Jessica came and met with me about her project last week," he paused for emphasis. "I think she is showing great promise and initiative... or maybe she's just looking for a raise." Jessica froze like a deer in the headlights. Her facial muscles were paralyzed. She felt like everyone was staring at her. Was she smiling? What was the look on her face?

Ken was delighting in her discomfort. "Are you looking for a raise, Jessica?"

Jessica tilted her head, scrambling for an appropriate way to respond. "Just trying to do a *professional* job." She narrowed her eyes at him for emphasis.

Ken laughed as if she had provided the perfect punch line to a wonderful joke and a few members of the team joined in. Charlene in particular seemed to find it funny, while Alan looked distinctly uncomfortable.

Jessica wished she could take back her response. In her imagination, she threw papers in his face and shouted "I QUIT!" and "You'll be hearing from my lawyer!" as she dramatically slammed the door – the glass in the door would shatter, of course. That's how things happened in the movies.

"In the next two months," Ken told her when the laughter died down, "we'll set your project up to present to the department heads. I want to fast track this through development and launch in time to announce at the annual company sales meeting."

Jessica nodded, still seething.

When the meeting finally broke up, Jessica forced herself not to run from the room. With her back deliberately straight, she headed for the door, only stopping briefly at her cubicle to drop her notes and grab her purse.

"Hang on, Jessica," a voice called.

Charlene had followed her. She had a smile fixed on her face and Jessica noticed Charlene's eyes rake up and down her body, critically. "Turn back around," she ordered.

Jessica did as she was told and felt a sharp tug followed by a *pop!* as Charlene yanked down on the hem of her new business blazer. Jessica realized the X thread must have still been on her jacket... She had taken off all the tags but had forgotten the damn X in the back.

Jessica turned to look at Charlene again. "Thank you." *You catty bitch.*

Jessica left the building under the umbrella of going out to lunch. She had no idea where she was going but she needed space to process what had just happened She drove her car to the coffee shop down the street and sat down with her cellphone in front of a steaming cup.

Liz had not forgotten the meeting. The text message waited impatiently on her screen. "How did it go?"

Jessica bit her lip. There were no words to describe how weird that meeting had gone. She knew there was no way to text it all. "Are you available to call?"

The phone rang half a second later and Jessica filled Liz in on the meeting, the weird public raise talk, and how much she had wanted to throw a tantrum and sue.

"We can have a nice long conversation about appropriate ways to leave a job but in short, you can't quit – not like that. You can't quit your way to success. So if you can get back to work this afternoon, let's focus on managing your boss. Are you going back to work?"

Jessica surprised herself by immediately answering, "Yes. I finally have a grasp on my project. I can see where it's going and I'm learning a ton. I can't quit now."

"Good. So it sounds like Ken has a management style that combines reward and punishment. Ken is probably not secure enough to be able to say good job without trying to humiliate you at the same time. Let me ask you this; do you admire Ken? Do you see him as a role model?"

Jessica thought for a moment and said, "No. I think he is rude, inconsiderate, and arrogant... but he's my boss."

"Exactly," said Liz, "so consider the source when you hear comments or remarks that seem rude or inappropriate. He can't get into your head unless YOU LET HIM IN. I know it's not easy and it takes a lot of breathing and thinking instead of feeling to keep yourself from imploding, but I know you can do it."

Jessica replayed the scene in her head again. "Someone at the table probably asked for a raise. He humiliated me to make a point to them."

"From what you've told me, it's not that far-fetched," Liz agreed. "I wouldn't put it past him at all. But now that you know his game, can you play it?"

Jessica realized she was nodding into the phone and verbalized her agreement.

Liz continued, "When you are in these meetings, think about all the elements you used to take a seat at the table. Remember, it's not literally a chair at the table that's important. Feel confident enough to take that seat and sit tall or stand tall – don't let these people take over the inner you. It's yours and yours alone... You are incredibly valuable and you never want to let it be controlled by anyone but you."

Jessica spent the next half hour breathing and thinking over her coffee, trying to wrap her mind around all that Liz had told her.

Note From Robbie:

In 2015 there was an article in the Huffington Post about a woman who was on the board of a public traded company who faced an unacceptable level of unconscious gender bias. This woman quit her job as a director at that company and went public with her story.

"The board assumed they knew how I would have voted based on a biased assumption that I'd vote to keep my 'friend'...Because that's what girls do, right? They make emotional decisions about friends instead of strategic decisions based on business facts... Had there been other women on the board, the decision to silence me would have been different... The more diversity, the more likely someone will speak up."

My reaction is, *why quit?* How do we change the game if we don't stay around and fight? Harvard Business Review published that once there are at least three women in a group, they "tend to be regarded by other board members not as 'female directors' but simply as directors. The women no longer report being isolated or ignored." So how can we get to three if the first one quits?

While Jessica's uncomfortable meeting was not out-right sexism, there is certainly an implied sexism that the comments were directed to her and not at a male colleague. Her boss deliberately tried to humiliate her, but to her credit, she is sticking it out. As Liz advised, you can't quit your way to success – and that holds true from team sports to the board of directors.

Chapter 7
Courting Change

The literacy center was located in a corner of the library and was crowded with pairs of adults hunched over books. Some were reading out loud, sounding out words as a child would. Others were writing and discussing their papers. The literacy coach would occasionally correct a word, or define one. Some were learning American trivia in preparation for their citizenship test and others were working from a VERY thick book, studying for their GED exam. There was incredible energy with a mix of fear as each person from 25–85 struggled to advance their lives through education.

It amazed Liz that every single chair was occupied by someone either learning to read, or write, or studying for the citizenship test or the GED exam, or someone coaching the process. When she had shown up unannounced to observe, the staff of the literacy center had told her that it was already full to capacity and that there wasn't a place available for her to work. She had assured them that it was okay, that she was just there to observe.

Liz shifted her legs slightly from where she had denned herself by a stack of old children's _Highlights_ magazines on the floor. It was easy to imagine herself as a nature documentarian sitting in a blind. _See the noble humans as they attempt to master words._

On her lap was a list of things she had observed. First and foremost, CHAIRS was in bold letters but the space was so small that chairs would be of limited use. The real issue was there was not enough physical space for the number of people seeking help. As she had grown more uncomfortable on the floor, she had first underlined and then circled the note. Included on the list were things like "larger space," "greater library of reading material," and "ample paper and writing utensils." It was amazing how basic some of these issues were...

She had noticed almost immediately that the bookshelves were close to bare. An inquiry with the staff had revealed that most of the books were checked out almost as soon as they were returned. There were some very basic readers, barely more advanced than board books, which permanently adorned the shelves. _See Jane Read_ was (understandably) not very popular with the adult crowd. There also did not seem to be any use of technology. Liz had found some free apps that provided Citizenship and GED flash cards. These types of solutions would certainly provide leverage for everyone.

As the groups of people teaching and learning shifted, Liz really wished Brad could be here to see it. She had spilled her enthusiasm to Brad over dinner the previous night, detailing the shocking illiteracy statistics and the non-profit she was devising.

He was also blown away, but he thought perhaps they should *donate to the cause* and not try to *actually solve the problems themselves.*

"I thought we were going to retire next year," were the actual words that had stung the most.

While her rebuttal had been true, that this wasn't going to be a full-time "corporate" project, with employees and investors, what she kept circling back to was the empty feeling in her gut when he had said *retire.* She could not envision retirement, the endless days of sitting on her hands, with no bursts of ideas and problems to solve.

If you got right down to it, after retirement things went roughly like this:

1. Retirement
2. Lots of travel
3. Doctor's Appointments
4. Moving to a Senior Community
5. Doctor's Appointments
6. Death or (worse) an awful nursing home

Brad really wanted to retire.

While the rational side of her brain knew Brad wanted to relax, see the world, and spend time together, the irrational side of her brain computed: Brad wants me to retire = Brad wants me to be like him. They had always celebrated their differences, but now it seemed like he was ready for her to be like him. For a moment, her irrational brain had been winning and she had actually been angry with him.

Liz did not understand why it had to be all or nothing. Semi-retired might work for her; she had plenty of viable time and energy left.

It hadn't been pretty from there. Although she thought she could retire AND run a non-profit, he didn't believe she could (and his disbelief had stung). The row had ended with an uneasy truce for her to review her plans and to circle back to the conversation next weekend.

A deep vibration pulsed against Liz's hip, causing her to start in surprise. Her body groaned stiffly at the sudden jerk, and a wave of pins and needles suddenly ran down her calves to her feet. She scooped her phone from her hip pocket. A text message from Brad. "Where are you? Evan's supposed to call in 5, remember?"

Crap! She had lost all track of time.

She slowly unwound her legs, gingerly stretching and wiggling her toes, feeling fresh waves of pins and needles. She hoped like hell she wouldn't need a hand to stand up (or worse, pitch over the second she was on her feet). She texted Brad, "Sorry! Lost track of time. Leaving now."

Liz managed to gain her feet by leaning on a wobbly bookshelf. It swayed forward and she pushed it back against the wall with a *bang!* before it could overturn. *Add wall mounts to the list,* she noted, nodding to the nearest literacy coach who looked up at the noise.

She managed to hobble her tingly feet out of the literacy center without tripping or otherwise making a fool of herself. The staff at the front had smiled politely at her as she said her goodbyes. Liz was quite certain they thought she was nuts for coming and just observing from the corner. Once outside she stomped her feet until the sensation had returned and she could trust herself to make it to the car.

Liz felt bad that she was missing the call with Evan. He had texted last night saying that he wanted to talk to them today. Liz suspected that he had finally gotten the promotion he had been talking about the last time he had visited. He and his wife, Ashley, lived in Southern California. He would need the pay raise to start a family in LA.

Speaking of money, Liz made a mental note to ask Jessica about her salary – she imagined she was at the low end of the pay scale for her job.

When Liz pulled into the driveway she could see Brad pacing in the kitchen with his hand to his ear.

She hurried into the house, hoping to catch the end of the conversation.

Brad was tall with dark hair fading to salt and pepper. He turned at the sound of the front door, revealing an ear-to-ear grin. He motioned to her with a, come here, come here, circling of his hand. "Hang on. Liz is here. I'm going to put you on speaker."

There was elation all over his face. "Just you wait! Just *you* wait!" After a moment of fumbling, the speakerphone squawked to life...

"Judging by your father's face, this is going to be good news."

Her step-son, Evan, laughed through the phone. "He never had a poker face!"

Liz could feel the giddy energy coming off of Brad in waves. She felt herself grinning and not even knowing why, though she could guess.

"Ashley is pregnant! We're going to have a baby!"

"I'm going to be a grandpa," Brad added proudly. Liz could see the tears welling up in his eyes and she loved him all the more for it. Evan was Brad's son from his first marriage and the two of them had always been close. Liz had met Brad when Evan was six years old and married Brad two years later. It had been a smooth transition. Evan was a joy to have for a stepson. And now she was going to be a grandmother.

Liz leaned forward and kissed Brad on the lips. "I'm so happy for you." She said this loud enough that Evan could hear her too. She was surprised to find that she was crying too and laughed, wiping her eyes.

"Grandma's crying," Brad informed the phone.

"Aw!" Evan crowed. "Telling people has been the best ever. Hang on, Ashley wants to talk to you too."

Brad snatched back the cellphone to talk to his daughter-in-law. He asked a number of questions of Ashley, like gender (too early), morning sickness (rough but manageable), and due date (seven months from now). Liz realized with astonishment that this was something Brad had anticipated, had even looked forward to eagerly. They wrapped up the call with another round of congratulations and 'I love you's.'

Brad pulled Liz into an embrace, squeezing her and kissing the blonde and white hair on her head. "We should get down to see them soon."

"Hmmm," Liz responded, not sure if this was a great idea. She tried to remember her own pregnancy and whether her own parents had swooped in. "I suppose we could go and spoil them rotten," she finally agreed, giving in to the excited feeling flapping around in her chest. *Children in the house again! WOOHOO!*

Note From Robbie:

I suffer greatly from the theory that "there has got to be a better way," and Liz demonstrates this in a subtle fashion as she looks at literacy training and how she can contribute and make it better. Most entrepreneurs do their best innovation from this vantage point.

New ideas and innovations are easiest when they are solutions to problems. Breaking ground and creating a market for a totally new thing is challenging... Innovators have a DNA that allows them to spot solutions often before they actually see the problem.

In 1975, Gary Dahl was in a bar listening to his friends complain about their pets. This gave him the idea for the perfect "pet": a rock. He sold 1.5M at $4/each. He solved a problem and created a new market...

The ability to step in or step out and change things takes solid self–esteem and gold–plated ovaries. The changes do not have to be as bold or public as this literacy program – in fact, they could be as simple as a new process or procedure at the office... The ability to feel confident is the key. That confidence comes from taking your seat at the table.

Chapter 8
Visualization

Jessica stood in the copy room before the big presentation, taking deep breaths, and singing to herself. According to Liz, if you sing, you have to breathe. Liz had told Jessica a story of when she was learning to ski, her instructor had taught her to sing songs from the _Sound of Music_ on tough slopes to help her relax... The theory was that singing required breathing and breathing makes you relax... and in Jessica's case, breathing reduces the chances of passing out from fright while public speaking.

Jessica was currently singing the lyrics to twinkle, twinkle little star. She could not think of a single song more dignified, and a remote part of her psyche noted (in a detached sort of way) that she had de-evolved to the mental equivalent of a preschooler.

I'm going to get myself fired. It was a thought that tried to insert itself as a lyric.

> *Twinkle, Twinkle Little Star*
> *How high is this latest bar?*
> *Is it really time to die?*
> *Will I bomb or will I cry?*
> *Twinkle, Twinkle Little Star*
> *Can I jump the highest bar!*

The small, detached voice in her psyche frowned at the lack of rhyming. Jessica fetched her phone from her pocket and dialed Liz.

"I am losing my mind," Jessica announced.

"Sometimes that is not a bad thing," Liz told her firmly. "You will look back at this and laugh, I promise."

"I'm going to get fired. Or worse, they are going to laugh me from the room."

"We'll examine your priorities later, but right now, take a breath."

Jessica obeyed.

"I can't hear you! Do it again!"

Jessica rolled her eyes, inhaled deeply and exhaled noisily into the phone. It was so silly that she found she was smiling and trying not to laugh at herself.

"Good. Did you do the visualization techniques last night?"

Jessica paused. Last night was the first time that Sarah had been home solo (*sans boyfriend* as they say) in days. They had laughed and had drinks until late. It had been great to reconnect, but no, she hadn't completed her visualization exercises.

Liz read into the silence and sighed. "Okay. Right now, let's do them. Close your eyes." Liz's voice changed, losing the business snap, slowing closer to a hypnotist at a fair. "Take a deep breath and let it out. Where are you?"

"In the presentation."

"You are calm. You feel light. You roll your shoulders down your back and hold your head high."

Jessica followed the directions subconsciously, feeling the muscles stretch as she pulled her shoulders down and tilted her chin upwards.

"Breathe in." Liz paused before directing her to breathe out.

"I want you to imagine yourself stepping down after the presentation. They are applauding. They are smiling and clapping. You have successfully presented your project. It is moving forward in production. It will be part of your product line. You are going to succeed. Can you see it?"

Jessica could both see it and see it failing at the

same time. Liz's vision was perfect and Jessica's subconscious tried to insert its fun little additions. There is toilet paper on her shoe. She trips and falls off the stage.

"Can you see it?" Liz asked again.

Jessica took a fortifying breath and pushed her subconscious to the side, letting Liz's vision solidify in her mind... "Yes."

"Good," Liz encouraged. "Your job is to go out there and articulate your vision for this product line. You have a great presentation. You are going to deliver it exactly like you practiced. You are going to break down the product line into its components, the problem in the marketplace, the space that this solution is going to fill. You are going to get people excited about this vision. You are going to succeed."

Jessica's imagination placed Liz's voice over her, speaking these words of encouragement and faith down upon her, like some heavenly voice of wisdom. She felt calm and told Liz.

"You go girl," Liz said before ringing off. Jessica rolled her shoulders back, checked the bottom of her shoe for toilet paper, and then held her head up high as she walked to the presentation room.

Jessica felt numb when she finished the presentation. She had stood in front of the major decision makers in the company and explained the details of the gap in the marketplace and where this product would fit. She had reviewed what would be required of each department to bring the product to market. Now she had opened the presentation up to questions.

Ken immediately fielded most of the questions. He was seated in the front row and turned to talk to the people behind him. His back was turned to her and she could only guess at his expressions as his head bobbed up and down, talking.

The entire product team was seated in the second row; they were ordered to come as a show of support. During the presentation it had been a bit weird to see them watching her doing the presenting. Now Jessica stood mute in front of them as their eyes flicked between her and Ken.

The back of the room was dim so her presentation would show up on the screen and no one had turned the light back on. Was that her responsibility? Somewhere in that dim light was the CEO as well as representatives from every other department of the company. Jessica's knees felt shaky with the spent adrenaline of fear and relief. She wondered if she could sit down now, or if that would be inappropriate. She no longer feared being fired. She wanted to turn on the lights.

Ken was fielding the questions but she was still paying attention to what was being asked. They had praised her, or her product line and initiative, at least. The tech department was stating some concerns and trying to find ways to simplify and do less in order to meet the timeline. The marketing department was claiming they didn't have enough time or manpower to put together the campaign the product would require. Ken had told her to anticipate that wrinkle, they wanted to push back by six months. To Jessica's relief, no one was saying, this is a stupid product or we don't need it... It was a purely a time and resources debate.

Jessica let her shoes take her to a seat in the front row. She felt like the weight and responsibility had lifted, she had taken the project this far and now Ken was shouldering it, at least for a short while. Alan leaned forward and gave her arm a squeeze. "Great job!" he whispered.

"Thanks." Jessica noted that no one else on her team even smiled her direction. They were now all focused on Ken as he wrapped up the Q&A session.

"Jessica? Where did Jessica go?" Ken asked, turning to look at the podium and the screen. He twisted about until he saw her farther along the row. "Why are you sitting? Stand up!" Jessica blushed and stood. "Look at her everybody!" Ken was grinning widely. "This is her very first project lead role! We need to give you a round of applause."

Ken started the round of applause by standing and clapping, then moved closer to her so that he was ostensibly receiving the applause as well. The meeting was over.

Outside of the conference room the CEO shook her hand and made some complimentary noises at her. Jessica had no idea what he said, she was a bit too stupefied to take it in. Charlene had caught it all though.

"Look at that!" Charlene exclaimed as she sidled up to her. "Rubbing elbows with the big guy." When Jessica didn't immediately reply, Charlene continued, "He was in town for the unveiling–ribbon–cutting thing for the Opera House. You know we sponsored a wing of the building right? I was surprised you weren't there. Ken and I had drinks with him after the ceremony."

"Oh," Jessica said. "I saw the email but I was rehearsing for the presentation and all that. I didn't think it was a big deal?"

"You should always go," Charlene advised. "Networking and free drinks. Unbeatable combination."

"Hmmm," Jessica nodded. She still thought she had made the right decision; she would run it by Liz sometime to see what she would have done.

Ken was suddenly there, all smiles and euphoria. He put an arm around each of their shoulders. "You should be best friends." Jessica had a flashback from a bar in college where a guy had done basically this same maneuver and then followed it up with, *You should kiss!* Jessica shrugged Ken off.

"Hey! Hey! You guys are going to be working closely together – you're team members! You should be friends."

Jessica was surprised to find herself asking Ken,

"Why didn't you let me answer the questions?"

"Oh, Jessica. I didn't think you were ready and I wanted to be sure we gave the answers the big boys wanted to hear," Ken laughed to emphasize his point and smiled at her condescendingly. "You will learn how to play the game, but you are not there yet. In fact, you are not even close."

Seriously?

Note From Robbie:

Visualization is a powerful tool. What you may not realize is that Jessica uses two very distinct versions of visualization in this chapter. The first is the exercise that Liz leads her through, to see herself giving a successful presentation. This exercise is internal to Jessica, getting her to relax and focus on a specific outcome – which she then achieves.

The second use of visualization is where visualization gets exponentially more powerful and difficult to achieve... Jessica's presentation is to communicate the value of her project, to present her vision of her product line, so that all stakeholders can "see" her project and understand what it entails.

This second form of visualization can make or break your career. When you can get everybody to see and share a single vision, you can do it. A strong vision and understanding of the objectives will keep your efforts focused and driven to achievement. You can accomplish almost anything if you can get everybody involved to see and understand it.

You will know when you have achieved this second form of visualization when your co-workers, colleagues, and stakeholders are able to share your vision and articulate it back to you. Additionally, when something's too complicated, you need to break it down into pieces. How your vision is regarded will tell you where it is succeeding and failing.

Chapter 9

BITCH

Brad has lost his mind.

Liz had been excited to hear she would have a grandchild. Brad had run out and bought a shirt that said, "Call me Grandpa!" He was wearing it now, as they drove the six hours to visit Evan and Ashley. He had subscribed to the kinds of newsletters that pregnant women get. Today he had informed her that Ashley's baby was approximately the size of a cucumber, and her uterus was approaching the volume of a Kleenex box. Liz couldn't shake the image of a Kleenex box poking her daughter-in-law's innards, while a cucumber grew in spirals within the confines of the rigid walls.

Liz tried to search back into her memory, to her pregnancy. Had Brad been so excited? Had her father? Liz only remembered the exhaustion and the overwhelming love for Marie. She supposed that Brad had been supportive, but did he run out and buy "Call me Dad!" shirts? Probably not.

Liz glanced at Brad from the driver's seat. *Who was this new person?*

"Slow down there, Hun. Traffic ahead."

He was right, a wall of cars had materialized up ahead. She had been zoning, musing on the stranger who had replaced her husband. She took her foot of the gas and slowly applied the brakes, matching the pace of traffic in front of her. A moment later, they were stopped behind a lifted Ford with a trailer hitch. The bumper sported a decal of Calvin gleefully peeing on a silhouette of a woman labeled *"all my ex's."*

"I hate L.A." Liz declared.

"We aren't even in L.A. yet," Brad pointed out.

"Exactly."

A flash of blue in the rearview startled Liz. The squeal of brakes came a heartbeat later. Liz reached out with her arm reflexively, as if it was 40 years earlier and Brad was a child riding unrestrained in a car. As if her arm could save him from harm.

"Hang –"

Her words were cut off by a crunch and then *bang!* as the speeding car rear–ended Liz's Honda and forced the hood under the trailer hitch of the lifted Ford. The world had gone slow-motion for Liz. She had time to briefly, hysterically, wonder if the last thing she would see was a vulgar bumper sticker, before the air bags deployed and she was suddenly enveloped in white and pain.

"Liz! Liz!"

There was a ringing in her ears, but Brad was calling her. That seemed good. Liz hadn't lost consciousness, but the world had taken on a fuzzy, remote distance... All urgency had been washed away.

"Yeah?" she asked, noticing a thickness to her voice. She tried to take a deep breath but it hurt.

"I think we're going to live."

"That's good."

The firetrucks and police came first. The ambulance medic passed over the blue car that had started it all in favor of Liz and Brad. The driver of the blue car was screaming at the top of his lungs about "that BITCH who slammed on her brakes," but it didn't seem very important to Liz at the time. It wasn't until much later, when all the shock had worn off that she realized he had been trying to blame the accident on her.

The momentum and angle had shoved Liz's Honda under the Ford's trailer hitch and then spun them when the hitch finally caught in the hood. The

Honda's driver's side door was roughly two feet away from the Ford's rear left tire. It took a while for the emergency crew to untangle the mess and cut her free.

Brad kept talking the whole time. "I love you," and "we're going to be just fine," were the common refrains. His door was unaffected by the crash and he was in and out of the cabin, talking with officials, making room for medics by coming around to her window. Later, Liz would think he had been everywhere, hovering over her. As the world came back into focus, and the pain sharpened, Liz was grateful for his love and reassurance.

All told, Liz thought they got off lucky. Her left wrist was fractured and splinted. Her nose was broken and the doctor had set it as best he could with the swelling. The arm she had thrown out to "Save Brad" was sprained and deeply bruised but not broken. She would take a good deal of ribbing from her husband and children over this in the next few weeks. Trying to protect a grown man wearing a seatbelt and facing an airbag by putting her puny old arm into the works. When Marie would call later, she would compare it to Wile E. Coyote being crushed between an airbag and an anvil. Liz felt bruised and swollen in every part of her body, but X–rays and an alphabet soup of tests had cleared her to leave the ER.

Evan and Ashley were waiting to bring them home. Liz couldn't remember crying at the scene of the accident, but she cried now... Ashley swollen with pregnancy and life, the concern of Evan for her and Brad... yes, the tears came now with relief and gratitude and emotions she could not yet identify. Later she would associate the feeling with the safety and love that only family and friends could provide.

Sitting immobilized by a heady mix of pain and narcotics on the couch, Liz noted ruefully that she and Brad had come down to shower love and affection upon their children. To spoil them and take care of them, only to have the tables turned. Ashley set up a TV tray in front of her with a steaming casserole and a glass of water with a straw. She pulled up a chair and picked up the fork.

"I guess this is going to be early practice," Liz sighed as Ashley prepared to fork food into her mouth.

"You've got to eat somehow," Ashley said lightly.

They were taking turns feeding Liz meals. Liz would have preferred Brad's help, it would somehow be less humiliating, but he was out with Evan buying paint for the nursery.

"I feel like we've stolen your thunder."

Ashley glanced down at her growing belly and touched it with her free hand. "It's exciting and at the same time, I wish people would stop staring. Stop asking questions."

"Brad's obsessed. The car accident might be a blessing so you don't have to discuss the size of your uterus."

"A Kleenex box." Ashley bit back a smile.

"Oh, he didn't!" Liz sighed, mortified.

Ashley started laughing and Liz winced when a chuckle contracted around the pain in her torso.

"Oh! Sorry. No laughing!"

"I'm sorry if he offended you," Liz said when the pain subsided.

"Brad's fine. He's excited for all the right reasons. It's the other people that really get on my nerves."

Liz felt her eyebrows furrow. "What other people?"

"Ever since I started showing, people feel totally free to say whatever they like, however inappropriate it might be." When Liz didn't say anything, Ashley hastened to explain. "Like a co-worker started advising me on what to eat. I'm a grown woman, you know?"

"Yeah, that's inappropriate. How's the HR department treating you?"

"That's been really good. Such a relief. My boss had a baby last year, so she's been super supportive. She's actually one of the few people I feel totally normal around. Like not everything revolves around pregnancy talk."

Liz racked her brain for something non-baby, non-car crash to change the subject to. The silence roared.

"Absolute strangers are the worst," Ashley mused. "The other day some guy came up to me and touched my stomach and totally tried to politicize my pregnancy. It was horrible. He congratulated me for taking a pro-life stance and started going on and on about dismembered babies being vacuumed up in utero."

Liz felt ill and wished desperately that she could protect Ashley from all the crazy people in the world. "What did you do?"

Ashley blushed. "I *lectured* him."

"Really?"

"Yeah. I told him to take his hands off of me. I shouted that of course I wanted my baby, I was having it, wasn't I? I yelled at him that I donate to pro-choice charities because a baby is a woman's choice. I have a *choice.* I told him to fuck off on the ignorant horse he road in on. And then he called me a bitch. I hate that word."

For a moment Liz glimpsed a bit of the strength that Evan had fallen so deeply in love with, and admired it... Ashley gave a rueful laugh. "There was quite an audience by the time I was done."

"Did he leave you alone after that? Or...?" Liz had a vision of a mob beating the crap out of this loser.

"Yeah. He said something about me being a hormonal bitch and he had been blessing me. When no one agreed with him, he turned tail and slunk away."

"Where was this?"

"The grocery store by my work. Evan offered to do all the grocery shopping from now until forever if it was too traumatizing, but he's calmed down now."

Liz smiled, remembering dragging Evan grocery shopping as a teenager, teaching him how to pick the ripe fruits and vegetables. She was very proud of her son for wanting to comfort his wife with ripe bananas and avocados, and for having the wisdom to not wrap her in a protective bubble.

"You know," Liz sighed, "I have been called a bitch so many times I've lost count. It's so stupid because really, it's not about me, or you; it's about the person so disempowered and threatened they are reduced to name-calling."

Ashley smiled in agreement. "In my experience outspoken women or assertive women are bitches. It's exhausting trying to fight that."

"It used to really bother me too," Liz conceded. "Years ago I decided to make my own acronym for it, to take the sting out. I finally decided bitch stood for, Beautiful, Intelligent, Talented, Compassionate, and Heroic."

"Does that work?"

Liz smiled, "Yeah."

For the rest of the afternoon, Liz regaled Ashley with stories of Evan. She hadn't been there until he was six, so there were no tales of potty training or spit up. She told Ashley about the Evan of his teenage years, as he began to form into the man she would one day marry.

When dinner was done and Brad and Evan called to say they were test driving replacement cars, Liz told Ashley about Jessica and the results so far of the mentoring project.

"Jessica is lucky to have you. I wish I had had access to someone like you when I was starting out."

Liz smiled thoughtfully.

Note From Robbie:

We all know that words can be very hurtful, but they seem to go hand-in-hand with growth and success. Those who can't "DO" resort to petty words. Successful women lean on the old adage of "consider the source," and when that fails the old nursery rhyme:

"Sticks and stones may break my bones but names will never harm me."

Words and labels have such power and we all know that women and men are labeled differently. Here are two examples:

Outspoken strong Woman = Bitch

Outspoken strong Man = Bold

Gray-haired Woman = Dumpy

Gray-haired Man = Distinguished

So rather than moan about how unfair this is, or let these labels define us, let's redefine them.

Maybe **POLITE** is really:

Paranoid **O**ffensive **L**oathsome **I**rresponsible **T**houghtless **E**gotistical

My point is that women need to understand the power of words and labels and how we react to them. So put that Beautiful, Intelligent, Talented, Compassionate, and Heroic brain to work on redefining those negative words and labels to what works for you.

Chapter 10

Pausing

Jessica eyed the ringing phone as if it would bite her. Nothing good had come from that phone in weeks. Her cubicle was littered with stacks of papers and notes and to-do lists for her current endeavor. At least this time someone was calling her, rather than the other way around.

She fought the urge to let the phone ring to voicemail and scooped it from the receiver. "Hello, this is Jessica?"

The ensuing conversation was painfully awkward. When it finally concluded, Jessica wanted to take shelter in the shadows beneath her desk. If she pulled her chair in after her, maybe no one would see her there, cocooning and praying to emerge as a less awkward form of existence. Maybe not a butterfly but–

"Was that a prospective supplier for your new product line?"

Jessica jumped and turned. Alan was peeking over the edge of the cubicle, smiling.

"Please tell me no one else heard that."

"A couple people walked by, but I'm the only one who stayed to listen."

Jessica couldn't decide if she was annoyed, humiliated, or defiant. She settled for curious. She couldn't beat her head against this wall forever. "What am I doing wrong?"

"Hard to pinpoint. Half the time you were trying to convince them that they needed our distribution channels. Half the time you were trying to mitigate the exposure if the whole project failed. You were planting seeds of doubt all over the place." His smile slipped a little. "I think you might need a book on negotiation. Maybe _Getting to Yes_?"

Or a mentor, Jessica thought. She made a mental note to call Liz and check in on her post-accident recovery.

"I'll Google it," Jessica stood up and stretched. "What brings you over from the cube farm? What can I do for you?" The cube farm was the company slang for the nestle of cubicles on the east side of the building. It received the bulk of the morning sun through large, wall-sized windows. Jessica's workspace resided on the other side of the building, called the Cubby Hole. There were no large windows

73

and no direct sunlight for the cubicle dwellers here.

Alan glanced around, ducking his head up and to the side to check for unwanted ears. It was almost five and weirdly empty. "Did you check your mailbox?"

Jessica quirked her eyebrow. Her email inbox was empty, she kept it immaculate as a form of procrastination. Alan meant their snail mail box adjacent to the HR department. "No... what's waiting there?"

"Management shake–up. Ken is still our lead, but things have shifted dramatically in other departments." Jessica felt her glasses shift as her eyebrows hit her hairline. Alan hastened to elaborate. "I'm sure it's fine. I just didn't see it coming. I had a transfer in and now it will probably get lost or denied. I was hoping you had heard something."

Jessica thought for a moment. She had no idea that Alan was trying to find a way out of the team, but she didn't blame him at all. "What are you going to do?"

Alan smiled sheepishly. "I think I'm going to get drunk and figure it out tomorrow. Want to come?"

Jessica froze.

"Oh!" Alan realized his mistake. "Not like that! I meant join me at the bar. With my girlfriend and a couple other people," he had started to stammer, blushing to his ears.

Jessica felt a wave of relief and disappointment... It was good to know where she stood, and she wouldn't have an office romance regardless, but she hadn't realized she liked him until now. She smiled reassuringly at Alan.

"Thanks for the invite, but I've got plans. Have fun, though."

The "plans" evolved quickly. It came into existence as an excuse, then reality when she picked up the ominous "notice of reorganized company structure" in her mailbox. She called Sarah and planned an impromptu pity party. Sarah obliged and somewhere in the blitzed out haze of tequila, Sarah announced she was engaged. More shots to celebrate!

Jessica woke up to a silent apartment. Sarah was gone, presumably to work. *Oh no! Work!*

She was an hour late and entirely immobile with self-inflicted sickness. She called in, knowing this would look horrible in light of the management changes but not seeing a better alternative. Ken, thankfully, didn't answer and she left a voicemail.

The kitchen was in shambles. In addition to empty bottles, sliced limes were dry and stuck to the cutting board. Someone had decided to make milkshakes and left the results in the blender. Jessica felt her stomach do a barrel roll. She pulled a water bottle out of the fridge and when she closed the door she saw a magnet featuring a kitten balanced precariously on a tree branch with the advice to "Hang in there!"

"Every day," she told the magnet and then scooped up the phone.

"You sound horrible," Liz informed her when she answered the call. "What happened?"

"Tequila. And maybe some milkshakes. I don't quite remember that part. Regardless, I thought I should check in. How are you feeling?"

"I'm still housebound. Don't change the subject. How is your project going?" Liz asked, displaying her uncanny ability to sense a problem.

"I'm not sure. Sometimes I feel like I am fucking up and other times I feel like I have things under control," Jessica confessed.

"Alright. You're obviously not at the office today. Come swing around and pick me up at my house. I need to get some sunlight and the doctor won't let me get behind the wheel of the car. You drive, I'll buy."

Ten days after the accident and Liz was still sore. They had bought one-way plane tickets home as Liz had been too sore to sit through a six-hour drive. The first few days had been a flurry of doctor's visits and insurance claims. Now her pain was accompanied with boredom.

Her home office was almost untouched. It hurt to sit too long at her desk and the pain pills made it difficult to form coherent thoughts. She had canceled her upcoming speeches; nose–broke, raccoon eyed, and bandaged was not the personal brand she intended to foster. The calendar forward was dismally empty, but the doctor would only guess at her recovery time.

"You are in good shape, for your age," said the doctor, who looked like the ink was still drying on his diploma... "But it is hard to put a timeline on these things."

Liz had roughly translated this to: *You're on the cusp of old age, lady, and some people never recover from this sort of trauma.*

The accident had created a sucking void of free time that was pulling her into a vortex between the TV and the kitchen. She would space out on pain pills watching daytime TV, only rousing when the pain threatened to break through the fuzz of the narcotics. She absolutely loathed the spiral, but whenever she tried to forgo the medication, the pain would grow teeth and start eating her alive, until she was snarling and biting off Brad's head ...

Jessica's call had been a relief. She needed to see sunlight and different faces from Brad and the talking heads on TV.

If she could have, she would have run out to Jessica's red Volvo and thrown herself into the front seat yelling, "DRIVE!" But as it was, she needed Jessica to help her into the seat and lean over her to buckle the belt. The fine motor skill of feeding herself (with her right hand at least) had returned, but exerting any sort of pressure with her fingers was agony.

"Physical therapy starts next week," Liz explained as Jessica withdrew from buckling her in. "It's supposed to be more painful than the accident, if you can believe the forums."

Jessica wrinkled her nose. "I wish there was something I could do to help."

"Take me away from this madness. I need sunshine and coffee and faces that don't belong to my husband or TV personalities."

They settled for lunch in a little café near downtown. Liz had requested an outside table, and marveled in the sunlight while Jessica studied the menu. Once the waitress took the order, Liz got down to business.

"No more avoiding, Jessica. What's going on?"

Jessica squirmed. "I can't seem to land a supplier contract. At all. This should be a slam-dunk, a win-win, and no one is signing. People are starting to notice. Alan was listening yesterday and he said I sounded like I was planning to fail. Like I didn't believe in my own project."

"Do you believe?"

Jessica considered for a moment. "Yes. I am just not communicating it. My pitch isn't working."

Liz asked Jessica to give her pitch. She did alright at first, but when Liz didn't say anything, she continued. She started to ramble. Then things really went off the rails. Finally, Liz waved her hands for Jessica to stop. "The good news is, you know your product line and what you're trying to achieve. The bad news is; you don't know how to pause."

Liz would later blame the pain pills, but she decided to tell Jessica *the story.* "This *does not* leave this table, okay?"

Jessica perked up, interested, "Okay."

"I was the CEO of a software start up, way back in the 90s and there was a company interested in buying us. The acquisition seemed to be a good opportunity for growth and a good return for the investors, but it was my first time selling my company and it is so different from doing mergers and acquisitions for other companies. So even though I had experience, I still had no idea what I was doing."

Jessica was nodding, listening closely.

"It was time for a final face-to-face meeting to try and hash out a deal. I wanted to bring our lawyer to the meeting, but we were on a shoestring and it broke the budget to pay for the airfare, hotel, meals, and his time. Now, in hindsight, I should have figured something out. Borrowed the money or gotten our lawyer to agree to be paid once we exited. There were options, but I didn't think about it.

"It wasn't until I was on the plane that I realized I would need a reason to pause in the negotiation meetings. There is this natural tension in doing deals and negotiations. The acquirer usually tries to exert pressure to close the deal fast. They want to get you caught up in the moment, but what you really need is a moment to consult the experts before you come back and answer.

"By leaving the lawyer at home, I realized that I had lost that opportunity. I kept trying to think of a solution, what could I use? I have no idea why, but I decided that I should try to find a Ouija board."

Jessica interrupted, incredulous. "In like a serious way, or like a –"

"In kind of like a tongue–in–cheek way. I couldn't say *I couldn't afford to have my lawyer come out here* – because they would decide to postpone the acquisition. Wait until you are financially desperate and then you have little to no room to negotiate."

"Right," Jessica agreed, "you're negotiating."

"Exactly. So I go to Toys 'R Us the next morning and there are no Ouija boards, but they have Magic 8–Balls. I bought one, left the packaging in the car, and shoved the ball into my briefcase.

"That's all the thought I gave to it. I didn't have

time. We get in the meeting. Things are cordial but tense. I'm trying to figure out how not to lose the deal. And they give me a number. And I can't talk about the number; because I signed, I can't disclose that."

Jessica nodded agreeably enough.

"So we're sitting there, and I said, I don't know, let me see. And I reached down into my briefcase, and I pull out this 8-ball, and I put it on the table. And I said, 'Let's see – since the lawyer's not here, let's see what the 8-ball says.'

"And in retrospect, I'm the luckiest person alive, because the two of them just started laughing. The CEO, grabs my hand and pulls me into his office up the hall. Right on his desk, he's got a Swami statue holding an 8-ball. This thing is BIG," Liz held a bruised hand over the table, estimating dimensions. "I've got this little black plastic 8-ball that we all know. And he's got this big, Buddha-looking guy holding an 8-ball. And he's like, oh, let's see what mine says.

"And then of course, I'm like, oh my God! What in the hell have I done? Anyway, long story short, he asked his 8-ball. I asked mine. You know how 8-balls give you no concrete answers.

"And then he said, okay, if you have the confidence or naiveté to come in here with a magic 8-ball, then I think you'll be a good addition to the team. And we agreed on a number."

"Fantastic."

"Yes, and no." Liz corrected. "It was fantastic because it worked. It was not fantastic because it was a VERY risky non-strategy. But!" She waved a hand dismissively. "Can you spot the lesson?"

"I need to pause." Jessica answered promptly.

"Exactly. You need to pause for you to consider, you need to pause for them to realize they really want the deal."

Jessica nodded to herself. "I can do that."

Note From Robbie:

The art of pausing mid-negotiation is a hard one to learn. It is like playing chess or a hand at poker. You need time to think through your moves. You also need time for your opponent to wonder what your full motives or potential is.

That may sound awful – a prospective partner or boss wondering what your motives are, but keep in mind, they are considering doing business with you. If you come in eager, you could appear desperate. If you come in with confidence, you grow in their esteem. They suddenly will invent other job offers, other business partners that may be interested in working with your company... Competition, imaginary or not, can only help your negotiating position.

One more benefit of taking a pause, is that you prevent yourself from making an emotional decision. You prevent yourself from taking the first offer. You prevent yourself from rejecting terms out of hand. You take the time to fully explore all the possibilities in your mind *and how you are going to express them, before continuing.* A pause will only raise you in their esteem, for your maturity, and the potential to use that skill to benefit their business in the future.

Chapter 11
Baby Shower

Liz was a bundle of nervous excitement on her flight down to LA. Her daughter Marie had coordinated her flight so they arrived at the airport within 30 minutes of each other. Marie was to chauffer her to and from Ashley's big day. It was a special treat for Liz to see both the girls in a single trip. She felt like it was her party rather than Ashley's baby shower.

At the airport, Marie bounded up and hugged Liz before she had hardly cleared the gate. Marie was a taller, darker haired version of her mother. While Liz knew it was absolutely ridiculous, seeing her daughter made her feel homesick for the days when Marie lived down the hall, shouting distance away.

Marie was like her mother in another way too.

She helmed a tech company. More specifically Marie ran an online app that monitored the users' health and wellness statistics. She regaled Liz with her war stories and victories on the drive through LA traffic.

Ashley looked absolutely adorable. She was six months along and was wearing her belly with pride... Standing among her friends, she radiated happiness and excitement. Liz snapped a picture to show Brad later.

Brad had been disappointed that men were not invited to the baby shower. She thought he might be the only man alive who wanted to sip tea and talk about pregnancy. But that wasn't quite fair. He didn't want to sip tea and talk pregnancy, he was just anxious to be *an active participant* in this next stage in his life. The strange rituals of women and their showers included.

"Are baby showers sexist?"

Liz had asked the question more to herself than anyone else, but one of Ashley's friends turned to her immediately to chat her up.

"I have wondered that too! It's such a catch-22. It's nice to have a proper shower, but feels so weird to hang out the 'No Boys Allowed' sign."

"My theory on showers, particularly bridal ones," Liz explained, "is that it is a special time to visit with the important people in your life before the big event occurs. Now that more men are taking paternity leave, helping with the parenting, maybe it is time to surrender the tradition."

"Absolutely not!" Marie exclaimed. "Men have had their clubs for years. YEARS! The golf club. The camping trips. The hunting! Times when they sit around and beat their chests and say, *Men! Aren't we great?* We women need to hang onto our traditions. Heck, we need more women-only traditions."

Ashley's friend gestured to the baby decorations, "And this one is the best, because Ashley is performing a damn magic trick. She's creating life. We've got to celebrate that!"

Marie chimed in. "That's right. Let's have a toast to Ashley's magical uterus."

Liz tried to hold back a laugh and managed a very unladylike snort. It kicked Marie and Ashley's friend into a fit of giggles. Then Liz couldn't help but join in too. Liz felt like maybe Marie had pushed it too far to get a rise out her mother, and of course had succeed to hilarious results. The rest of the guests were beginning to look over at the laughing trio.

Ashley came over, "What's so funny?"

Liz was trying to catch her breath, and wipe her eyes. "Nothing," she tried to hold her face straight. "It's just a magical party." And they were off again into another laughing jag. Ashley looked at them like they were a bit crazy, but smiled good-naturedly. She knew her guests well enough that the laughter wasn't mean spirited.

Liz and Marie spent the rest of the party chatting

with Ashley's friends. She did herself proud in the shower games, and won a Baby Ruth candy bar by diapering a tattered cabbage patch doll the fastest. The gifts were an orgy of tiny clothes and diaper cream. Some of the more useful items were gifted in duplicates, and the group teased Ashley that she and Evan had set up competing gift registries rather than coordinating their efforts. Liz felt a bit sorry for Ashley that she would have to haul all that loot back to the store to return it. She made a note to chide Evan into helping her, since his "help" had created the situation.

Exhausted, sore, and happy, Liz boarded a late flight home that night. She was glad she had made the trip for the shower. Silly tradition or not, it was important to shower Ashley (and by proxy, Evan) with love.

Note From Robbie:

Men have been going on boy's trips for centuries, hunting, sports, bachelor parties, etc., while women kept the home fires burning... Women's trips are a more recent phenomenon; weekends away at the beach, in the bar, shoe shopping, hiking, etc. It is still very new and evolving in scope.

Gender-specific isolation isn't the norm (and shouldn't be) but it can be a special haven. These siloed activities are bonding experiences. Bonding is empowering. Both men and women need to feel empowered and now women are realizing just how important those girls-only events are to their life and to their career.

A number of women feel uncomfortable with hanging out the No Boy's Allowed sign. They've fought for inclusion and now specifically dis-including men seems taboo. However, if you've ever walked into a room where you are the minority, where you are subtly questioned about your qualifications or your right to be there, it might be a relief to have a network where you 100% belong.

Women-Only networks create a place where we can nurture relationships in a way that feels comfortable, in a venue where we make the rules, and in a private space that empowers us. While the benefits of Women-Only networking have only recently been a topic of study for academics, all early indications are that women-only groups provide huge social and career benefits to the participating women. I would encourage you to go find out for yourself!

Chapter 12

Negotiating

Ken frowned as he looked through Jessica's report. She sat across the desk fidgeting in her chair. He looked up, still frowning.

"Why do you think you are getting a such a poor response?"

"I've thought a lot about that. It's a great opportunity and partnership." She shook her head for emphasis. "All of the contracts I've managed to get signed are very happy to be involved. I'm not sure the decision makers at these other companies are even getting the message that we want to talk. Like their gatekeepers are overzealous or something."

Ken smiled. 'Overzealous gatekeepers' was

something he would say. Jessica had used it purposefully because Ken liked to think he was molding and grooming her. In actuality, Liz had helped her frame how she wanted this meeting to go. Now her chance had arrived.

"Obviously we need more partners to make this work." Ken sighed and tilted back in his chair.

"I was doing some research on how to catch these decision makers away from their gatekeepers," Jessica strained to keep the nervousness out of her voice. If she gave away how much she wanted this, he might say 'no' just to show off his power. "There's a conference coming up next month. All of the major players will be sending representatives. I'd like to go and make the connections in person."

Ken considered her quietly for a moment. He was leaning so far back in his chair that he appeared to be looking down his nose at her. She held his gaze, refusing to fidget, look away, or back down.

He inhaled deeply and shot forward to his desk, laying his forearms on his desk and pressing his chest forward, like a cat about to pounce. "You already know that there are a group of employees going to the conference."

"Yes."

"They can't make these connections for you?"

"No, because they don't know the new product line as well as I do and this is my project."

He squinted in thought. "Officially, you're going to strengthen the relationships you've forged, put faces with contracts, press the flesh." Jessica was trying not to smile when Ken fixed her with a pointed look. "I need you to deliver on your idea."

"I'll start letting my contacts know I will be there."

Jessica stood up to leave but Ken wasn't done. "You'll find most of the contacts you want to meet will be available after hours in the bar. Make sure you wear something appropriate. I'll let Charlene know you're going to need some help."

She flushed, completely dumbstruck. *Did he really think she didn't know how to dress for a bar? What exactly did he expect to happen at this conference?* And for a moment she thought, *is this sexual harassment?*

She was rooted to the spot. Ken's eyes were twinkling and Jessica found that she was angry. Furious. She forced air into her diaphragm.

"I'm not sure I get your meaning, Ken." She forced herself to sit. She was not going to be criticized about her looks, while standing in front of him like a student in the principal's office... She wanted to scream at him. She wanted to rage, but she wouldn't give him the satisfaction. In fact, since she sat back down, Ken had gotten distinctly uncomfortable.

"Business casual can be a hard note to strike. Especially at a conference." His eyes were darting towards the door, willing her to go or maybe willing someone to come in and interrupt.

"Business casual," Jessica forced herself to take a casual tone. "That's good to hear. For a moment it sounded either like you think I'm too trashy, and need to button up, or that you would like me to get trashy to attract the attention you want. Obviously, that would be inappropriate."

Ken gave her a greasy smile, "Put away your feminist war drums, Jessica. I'm just trying to help you."

"Maybe. But it's coming across as something else altogether."

Ken rolled his eyes and sighed, "Get over yourself."

Jessica gave him a flat stare. "I don't think Charlene's input will be necessary."

Ken shrugged. "If that's what you want."

Jessica stood up, "It is."

She had planned to call Liz right away with the results of her meeting, but now she needed to think about her entire conversation with Ken and what did it all mean. So instead she called Sarah from the privacy of her car to sound it out.

"Congrats! Conference time!" Sarah exclaimed.

"I'm not so sure anymore," she related the end of the conversation with Ken.

"He probably doesn't want you to wear a miniskirt and be too sexy."

Sarah had been completely wrapped up in wedding planning lately; it actually felt weird to have a non-wedding conversation. On top of that, Sarah seemed to be purposefully missing the point. She was spinning the situation into the best possible light. "What are you going to do while I'm out of town?" Jessica tried to keep her voice light.

"Oh, I was thinking of inviting my mom to town so we could try on wedding dresses." A piece of the puzzle clicked into place. Sarah's mother was very budget conscious. Obviously by timing the trip for the same weekend as the conference, Sarah planned on "saving" her mom the hotel costs, by offering her Jessica's bed – so that money would be applied to the dress budget. Sarah's "advice" was based on her wanting Jessica out of town for the weekend.

Jessica tried to sort out what she was feeling. Betrayed. Sad. Too exhausted to fight. "Sounds fun. I gotta go. Meeting starting." She hung up and stared out into the parking lot. Her phone buzzed with a text message from Liz.

"Sooooo?"

Even though she felt like crying, she replied, "Conference! ☺"

Note From Robbie:

As a child, if I was rude, used forbidden words, or talked back to an adult, a soapy washcloth was the antidote... My mouth was swabbed out with soap and water to "cleanse it" of my impure words. It worked for about a week until I forgot and opened my mouth again without thinking about the consequences.

My parents wanted their daughters to be very polite and respectful. Most parents want polite and respectful children, but I think daughters get an extra dose or two of polite – while sons get by with the "boys will be boys" pass. The over emphasis on girls being polite can stay with us throughout our lifetime.

This early politeness training drives a certain part of the discrimination that occurs in the home and the workplace... Women often feel like they can't speak out. Or that they need to explain themselves in copious detail – how or why they reached a conclusion, how thoroughly they researched it... and then are interrupted by their male colleagues. Most men have been conditioned that interrupting is not impolite but just part of the process of life. Is it impolite? Is it disrespectful?

It doesn't actually matter. The point is that you have permission to:

1. Speak up or disagree without any extra words – make your point in as few words as possible.

2. Don't whisper or talk so softly that no one takes you seriously.

3. Interrupt – it's okay to interrupt, but you must acknowledge to yourself that you are interrupting so you are prepared for any blow back.

4. Eliminate "Just" from your vocabulary – a word that is often used to make yourself small and inconsequential, i.e. "I just want to ask a quick question." Or "I just need to check this detail…"

5. Throw the soapy washcloth in the incinerator and say what's on your mind, without preamble and without excuses.

Chapter 13
Extend a Hand

"Sorry I'm late, traffic was a bear," Liz said as she slid onto a stool at Harry's, a lovely downtown wine bar.

Nancy looked up from her phone and smiled, "No worries, I already ordered for both of us."

Liz was so grateful to be off of the pain pills. It made happy hour with friends possible again. She took a sip of the proffered glass of cabernet sauvignon, and complimented Nancy on the choice.

Nancy had moved to town about five years ago with her husband, Frank. Liz had met Nancy at a speaker's forum and taken a chance on the tiny, tough-as-nails lawyer... She had come through beautifully, negotiating the best possible outcome,

ROBBIE HARDY

and a friendship built on respect had flourished out of it.

"So, tell me about the baby shower, Grandma!"

Liz couldn't help but smile. Nancy had three grandkids that she doted on. No one was more excited about the impending arrival (and new title for Liz) than Nancy.

Liz filled her in on the exciting day in LA and turned the conversation to Nancy's arena. "How about the literacy center. What's going on there?"

It had been Nancy who had invited Liz into the literacy conference months ago. After moving to town, Nancy had thrown herself into the community, becoming active on several boards and service groups. It created business for her, but it also gave her a sense of purpose beyond litigation.

Nancy frowned. "We're planning another conference again for next year. They are trying to expand the scope and fundraising aspect. I'm having trouble getting traction with potential sponsors."

"Why do you think that is?"

"Well, the usual suspects are on board. They are always good to us. I just am having trouble getting my foot through the door with a few of the bigger employers around here."

Liz thought for a moment. "Are you looking for sponsorship for straight cash donations, or for exposure, or in-kind gifts?"

Nancy looked at her, her face inscrutable. "Damnit Liz, why do you always have the answers?"

"What?"

"You're right. I don't need cash. I need exposure. I need attendance."

"Alright, now we're talking." Liz pulled out her phone and Nancy and Liz ran down the list of contacts, discussing which ones could be approached for marketing and how to frame it. When they were done, Liz emailed over the few names and contact numbers that Nancy thought would be the most help.

"You know, Liz, you are different then a lot of people out there."

"How do you mean?"

"People aren't like you. When I moved here you welcomed me with open arms when other people looked at me like I was a charity case. People would treat me like 'what do you want' when I would try to talk to them. You have always approached me with 'what can I do for you.' It makes it so easy to be your friend."

"I didn't realize you had such a hard time when you moved here. I'm sorry."

Nancy laughed, gesturing her hand as if to brush the apology away. "Change is hard, but worth it. I'm nearer to my grandkids, and business is better here than it ever was in Tahoma. And the weather," she sighed dramatically, "is worth all the social anxiety in the world."

Liz thought about her conversation with Nancy on her way home. She wished that more people could extend a hand.

Note From Robbie:

When I moved to Napa I did not know anyone. I deliberately set out to find a network of like-minded women to befriend. When a series of circumstances led to an invitation to join a group of local very successful and interesting women, I was very flattered and very excited.

My flattery and excitement were short lived. As I began to reach out to these individual women to get to know them better, they questioned my objective. Basically they suspected I had ulterior motives - that in fact, I was trying to use their network and connections, or pump them for a job! Instead of seeing me as someone new in town, 3000 miles from my friends and connections, they were operating on a level of suspicion and mistrust. Would no one extend her hand to me?

Luckily, I found another group of women. Women who were open to friendship, open to expanding their social circle, willing to extend a hand. These women have been wonderful to get to know, and yes, we have passed business and made introductions for one another - along with restaurant recommendations and all the other things you need to know in a new community. The women of this second group have helped me make Napa my home.

Bottom line, there are women who could use the benefit of your knowledge and generosity, if you are willing to share it. We are never too old, too fat, too thin, too busy, too young, too anything, to extend a hand to another woman. Will you join me in this journey to extend a hand to another woman?

Chapter 14
Spa Day

When Jessica began to prepare for her trip, the work bit was easy. Flights were booked, emails were sent to clients inviting them to meet, and messages were sent to prospective clients as a pre-introduction. As far as the "girly stuff" went, Jessica was completely clueless. After several attempts at googling – and ending up completely overwhelmed, she wrangled Sarah into picking a spa and booking the appointments – under the guise of checking venues for possible wedding prep activities.

While Jessica was sick of hearing about wedding details, she was happy that Sarah decided to set spa appointments for them both. Sarah had decided that she must look her best for dress shopping, so they had joint haircut and wax appointments. Jessica wasn't sure what Sarah would do when she was getting a massage, but it probably would involve champagne. The drinks would make the girl-talk more fun. It felt like forever since they really talked.

So it was with a bit of dismay that Jessica realized that Sarah had brought a stack of bridal magazines into the spa.

"I wanted to show you this bridesmaid dress," Sarah opened a magazine to a dogeared page.

Jessica looked less than enthusiastically at the pastel floor length dress with spaghetti straps worn by a simpering model... "What else do you got?"

"Not the color, of course! The cut. You have to use your imagination!"

Jessica rolled her eyes and then looked at the picture again. "Sure. In black. With rhinestone and press-on tattoos of dragons."

"Don't be difficult."

"Don't be a bridezilla. You know I'll never be able to pull off spaghetti straps. My shoulders are huge. Spaghetti belongs on a dish, not a dress."

"I'll find something," Sarah grumbled as she disappeared behind her magazine.

Jessica leaned back onto her lounge chair, feeling sad and lonely. Her friend had disappeared down a wedding black hole. She wondered how long until her first appointment, so she could have someone to talk to. When the waitress came by, she ordered a cocktail. If it was going to be a wedding talk day, she would need to be well lubricated.

When Jessica came back from her massage, Sarah was sipping a drink, flipping idly through her magazine. Jessica caught the headline of an article as Sarah turned the page.

"Are you changing your name? What is Ryan's last name, anyway?"

Sarah wrinkled her nose. "Browning."

"Sarah Browning?"

"I don't know. Is that any better than Sarah Simmons? The whole name thing is such a big decision."

Jessica frowned. "It seems like giving up your identity."

"Yes. I got an MBA as Sarah Simmons. I ran a half marathon as Sarah Simmons. I am Sarah Simmons. So does that change when I commit my life to Ryan? I'm no longer Sarah Simmons, but Sarah Browning?"

"So... keep your name?"

"Maybe – but then am I not committed according to the traditionalists. My parents got a divorce, but they are all for traditional roles, which is weird. My mom took my dad's last name and made her last name into her middle name. If I do that, I'm Sarah Simmons Browning... Or hyphen Simmons-Browning."

"That's a mouthful."

"And then if we have kids – and kids are totally in the plan – are they hyphens? Because that's a lot of spelling for a little kid. That's like," she paused to do the math, "15 letters plus whatever his or her first name is. That's too much. So are they Browning even though I'm not a Browning? It all seems so needlessly complicated."

Jessica wasn't sure what the answer was, but she was happy to hear that Sarah was thinking about her identity. Maybe she hasn't completely lost herself down the wedding black hole after all...

Note From Robbie:

Roberta Frances Ball is the name my parents gave me. They only used all three names (with their voice raised) when I was in trouble. I consider it my given name, my birth name and yet when I was probably eight years old I had a crush on a boy and I began to write Mrs. Larry Abramo (in cursive) all over my book covers and papers... I was ready to abandon MY name completely because I was in "love" – WOW.

The notion/tradition that a woman will change her name when she gets married has many undercurrents that I think deserve our attention. We tell little girls you can be anyone or anything if you study hard, do your homework, and listen to your parents: BUT you might need to change your identity depending on whom you marry and in what generation of "tradition." SERIOUSLY?

We tell these little girls that they are important, that they matter, that they have value. We tell them they are more than a daughter or a wife or a sister or a mother. We tell them they are a whole person all by themselves. Yet when these same women are married, they are faced with adopting an entirely new name or rejecting a tradition. Rock, meet hard place.

As we work hard to make women truly equal (in all senses of the word) I think this name change tradition is archaic. While it is romantic to an eight-year old with a crush, it is time for the name change flag to come down. Let's all keep our own names unless there is a legal, cultural, or religious reason for changing it...

P.S. Full Disclosure: I did indeed change my name when I got married in 1967. When I got divorced in 1974 I did not change my name back, but rather kept my first husband's name, as that was now my true identity. I had worked hard to make a reputation for myself as Robbie Hardy, and I would be Robbie Hardy forever more.

Chapter 15

Networking

Jessica wondered fleetingly if she was depending on Liz too much. If she was being a burden. She almost put the phone down but her treacherous fingers hit "Call" instead.

Liz, as always, was soothing, understanding, and a fount of wisdom. "Networking is hard," Liz agreed. "There's just no two ways about it. Anybody who says it's easy and they like it all the time I think is lying either to themselves or to others, because it's hard."

"Which part do you think is the hardest?" Jessica asked out of morbid curiosity.

"I think walking into a room where you don't know anyone with a stack of business cards in your hand is tough in itself. You have to try and assess the room and find the right people to meet, while not wasting tons of time with people looking for jobs or trying to sell you something, cause that's what happens."

Jessica pondered this for a moment. The hardest part for Liz was finding the right people to talk to. She thought about all the networking events that she had gone to and stood anonymously in the corner, not speaking to anyone.

"Now I believe, that there is never a wasted moment in networking, because I always ended up getting something out of it. Even if it was small, it might lead to something else. And it was good for me even though I often hated it."

Jessica suspected that Liz had added that last bit for her benefit. She couldn't imagine the commanding speaker she had met while networking hating it at all. She couldn't imagine Liz doing anything she didn't want to do.

"What is the hardest part of networking for you, Jessica?"

"Walking in," Jessica said promptly.

Liz laughed on the other side of the line. "I totally get it. I would sit in my car and I would think, I'm here but I don't know anyone in there. No one is expecting me. No one will know if I don't go in, except of course me. And then I'd pep talk myself and bully and tell myself things like, well why did you bother to drive 30 miles and research who would be here? Get in there!"

"I usually leave," Jessica confessed.

"But not always," Liz reminded her. "So let's say you make it through the door. You finally overcome all of that and you meet some people and it's awkward and it's difficult. But you learn. And it's a lot of small talk. And your face is *so* tired of smiling."

Jessica tried not to smile at how true that was.

"Here's the interesting thing about networking: I think it is circular. When you look at networking diagrams, it's generally one person and lots of arrows out to other people connecting. And it never goes back. That's not the way the networking world really works, nor should it.

"It has to be circular, because I meet you. You help me. I should be thinking about if I can do anything for you. Maybe not today, but maybe down the line. You keep track of all the people you meet in some form or fashion that works for you. Then when something comes up and you're trying to think, oh, who could do that? It's like, well Jessica does that. I met her three years ago. Send her an email and see what comes of it.

"Do you get what I mean? If you connect people together, if you ask people what they need and if you connect them to someone helpful, you are giving. That circle revolves around you. You are creating a circle of people helping one another and what goes around comes around."

"So, at the conference I shouldn't try to get the contracts?"

"No. You are going to network to meet people. Ask them questions and listen to the answers. If you put their agenda first, their needs first, that's what makes an impression. If you walk up to someone trying to get a contract, they are going to keep you at arm's length.

"Try to see what you can do for them, which in turn, they may be more receptive to you. It's all little steps forward."

"My co-worker Alan has a whole strategy worked out. He has a key idea of how many business cards he wants to get and to try to set appointments for 30 min coffees where he can sit down and get them to know, like, and trust him. Do you think I need to do that too?"

"In a conference setting, absolutely. You should have targeted three to four people that you want to try to get an appointment with. But here's my caveat. Don't force them to set the appointment during the networking. Take a card, write a note, ask for a preference on how to contact whether they like calls, email, texts, whatever."

"Why?"

"Well, two reasons. Picture yourself networking.

What's in your hands? Cards? Wine? Food? It's very cumbersome and awkward to juggle all of that. You can barely shake hands and swap cards, let alone, let me look at my calendar on my phone now. It's going to frustrate me if you push me to drop everything to accommodate a meeting **for** you.

"The other reason is that you want to build trust. You are going to say, 'I'll contact you tomorrow.' When you do, you have credibility. You are already demonstrating that you say something and then you follow through. Makes sense?"

"Yes." Jessica allowed herself to feel a little more hopeful.

"So do you feel a little more comfortable about it?"

"Getting there. Technical skills question. When you walk into a room there are little cliques of people and you've got a few wallflowers standing on the side of the room. What do you do?"

"I go up to a clique of people, usually. And introduce myself. If the circle feels closed, I don't let it stop me. I just wiggle in and say, 'Hey, I'm Liz from Wherever Inc., how are you?' And you'll be surprised. That group will open up to you."

It was exactly the answer Jessica suspected it would be. But her stomach clenched at the idea of approaching a group. She usually just talked with the other wallflowers.

"It's an interesting point that you bring up," Liz

mused. "Yes, I tend to go to the clique first. I've certainly walked up to individuals but it's rare. I think I probably am a snob to them. I'm thinking, 'get your shit together.' I don't know. It's always a concern that someone on the outskirts will latch onto you and potentially drag you down and waste your time. You're stuck with that person.

"I wouldn't have approached you, Jessica. But I do hand it to you. You found a moment when you were comfortable talking to me, in the lull. And you made a good impression and didn't over-extend yourself. I'm really glad that you did too."

Jessica blushed into her phone. She was the lucky one here.

Note From Robbie:

I have spent a great deal of my professional life networking. It certainly was not easy and I can remember many times when I would sit outside an event in my car and say to myself...*no one knows I am here, so if I don't go in, it doesn't matter...* Those of us who have done a lot of networking can tell you it gets easier, and it does, but there are days and times where it is just plain HARD. However, the benefits can be huge, and let's face it, to some extent networking is a numbers game.

There are many books on networking and you can easily spend more time learning how to network than to actually doing it. You have to shake a lot of hands, talk to a lot of people, and drink a lot of mediocre wine before you are going to find the gems in every room... I'm not here to coach you on the "in–room" part of networking, but to encourage your post–networking habits.

The secret to my networking success is in the follow up. I keep track of my connections, I add them to my contact list, add them to LinkedIn, send thank you notes, set follow–up meetings, and in general try to maximize the connections that I made at each networking event. By fostering these relationships, I can not only get the word out about myself and my business, I can also learn about theirs. As I meet more and more people, I can see how introducing and connecting people with complimentary products will help them succeed as well. Successful networking isn't just about directly forwarding my business. It's about a rising tide raising all boats. If making introductions leads to business wins, then I'm raising the tide for everyone.

Chapter 16
Labor Pains

Liz hung up with Jessica and turned the treadmill back on. Her physical therapy had hurt like a mother in the beginning, but now Liz felt reenergized by the physical exercise. The endorphins were addicting and she was starting to see a tone to her muscles that hadn't been there since her 40s. She had even paraded and flaunted her reshaped figure for Brad, to their mutual satisfaction.

Brad was futzing around the house somewhere now. Liz hoped he had a plan for dinner (it was his turn to cook), and then let her mind wander to the problem of Jessica. She was ridiculously smart and terribly self-conscious. What was it about smart girls? Why were they so scared to shine? Had she been afraid to shine? She did not think so, but it was a different time and culture.

Liz was not sure Jessica had ever really been comfortable in her own skin. A thought nudged at Liz, not quite revealing itself but teasing her at the back of her mind. She kicked up the treadmill speed to see if the endorphins could kick the idea loose. Whatever the idea was, it would remain nebulous for a time yet, but Liz did acknowledge that she was determined to help Jessica get comfortable with Jessica. Self-esteem, self-acceptance was, after all, one of the keys to success.

She brainstormed to the whir of the treadmill. When Brad banged open the door in excitement, Liz had entirely forgotten that he was home. She started badly, missing a step and then scrambling wildly to stay on the speeding treadmill. The rubber rushed in its endless loop and Liz wheeled her feet furiously to keep from tumbling off.

Brad made an inarticulate noise, like a goat caught in a fence as he rushed over and slapped at the console, trying to slow it down and rescue her. On the third try his hand finally connected with the right button and the treadmill wound down to a hum.

Liz and Brad panted into the silence. After a beat, Liz grinned. Brad wiped his brow with the back of his hand and pitched his voice up high in a Ricky Ricardo impression, "We were almost in *big* trouble there, Lizzy!" They both laughed like loons.

When she finally caught her breath, Liz asked, "What's got you so worked up?"

Brad started, this time slapping his forehead with the heel of his hand, "Evan called! Ashley's in labor!"

"Really?"

Brad swept his arms around Liz and began dancing her across the floor. "You dance wonderfully, Grandma." He spun her out and then back, then leaned her into a gentle dip, mindful of her healing injuries.

"Fancy footwork there, Grandpa."

"How soon will you be ready to go?"

"I've got to shower. Pack. Send a couple emails."

Brad frowned. "You shower, I'll pack, you send emails from the road?"

Liz could feel his need to get on the road, the draw of the imminent grandchild that could not be put off, and she relented. She wanted to meet her grandchild too. They were on the road in less than an hour.

Brad drove like a teenager, making the six-hour drive in five. Liz had forced herself to stop watching in the first hour when Brad made an abrupt lane change and had been chastised by a chorus of angry horns. She spent the first half of the trip writing down some thoughts about Jessica and the similar Jessica's she had mentored during her career, their similarities and common issues.

The nebulous thought from the treadmill was still elusive, but she felt like the notes might coax it along.

When the battery on her laptop ran low, she resigned herself to singing to the radio and staring off to the distant hills. She wondered how the people in those hills made their money and spun business ideas for the region. Liz was vaguely aware that this was not normal for most people, but it was comforting for her. Her whole world seemed to be trying to get somewhere safely tonight and none of it was within her power. Ashley, the baby, Brad, the car, her health, she could worry herself to death if she wasn't careful. Instead she planned out horse ranches, orchards, and wind farms for anonymous hill dwellers.

They drove straight to the hospital. Evan had been silent since his initial call and neither Brad nor Liz wanted to bother him now. He was either holding his wife's hand or his baby, and nothing should come between either responsibility. After checking in with security and attaching visitor badges for the maternity ward, they anxiously inquired after their daughter-in-law at the nurses' station.

The nurses glanced at each other, smiling. A tickle of intuition let Liz know that something was up, but whatever mischievousness had passed between them was secondary to their professional duties. It would not exist without a healthy mother and baby. Liz suddenly teared up. *Baby...* He or she had arrived...

Evan materialized behind them. He was grinning

manically. There were hugs and tears. Liz marveled that she was crying in happiness for Brad, Evan, and Ashley, in relief for a safe delivery of a grandchild, and in love for someone she had never met but dreamed of. She pawed back the tears in her eyes and found Brad and Evan doing the same.

"Boy or girl?" Brad asked, grinning and wiping his eyes.

"Come see!" Evan beckoned them down the hall.

They entered the room, but the bed was obscured by a curtain. "Ashley, they're here. You ready?" Evan called softly through the curtain.

"Yes. Let them through," came a tired, smiling voice.

Evan pulled the curtain aside with a *tah-dah!* flourish. Ashley lay propped into a sitting position in the hospital bed. Her arms were each occupied with a receiving blanket bundle. Liz glanced quickly between the two, trying to figure out which one of the bundles was the baby. When it finally clicked home, her knees felt weak and she found herself seated abruptly on a chair she must have only sensed subconsciously.

The double baby registration list "mistake." The refusal to reveal the gender to anyone. The glance between the nurses.

Ashley and Evan were grinning expectantly at her and Brad. She found she was grinning back. "One's a boy and one's a girl, isn't it?" Evan's eyebrows shot up in surprise but Ashley just grinned and nodded.

"You little stinkers!" Brad crowed. "Give one here."

In short order Brad and Liz each held a grandchild. Liz found she could not look away, could not take her eyes off this perfect little bundle. The perfect arc of eyelashes, the translucent delicate nails, the way the eyes twitched as they dreamed beneath closed eyelids. She wondered for the first time in 30 years what a baby could possibly dream about. But here she was, hours new to the world and dreaming her baby dreams. She ached to pull off the pink cap that announced she was a girl, to inspect each individual hair on her head. Liz had no name to call her granddaughter yet, so she was *Beautiful* and *Precious* in her mind.

Liz didn't get a chance to hold her grandson that day. There were nurses in and out, doctor's tests, babies to feed and change. Once her granddaughter was taken out of her hands, she busied herself taking pictures and making conversation. Soon Ashley's mother and step-father would arrive from Scottsdale, and Liz wanted to be gone before they arrived. She didn't trust that she wouldn't blurt the secret in the hallway and ruin the surprise that Evan and Ashley had cooked up for nine months.

Evan walked them to the elevators. "You'll be staying in town for a while, right?"

"We're checking into the nearest hotel." Liz

assured him. She couldn't imagine a prolonged drive again anytime soon.

Evan nodded. It occurred to her how difficult this had been for him. To stand helpless as his wife grew, and widened, and finally unleashed life into the world. Evan looked like a man who had lifted the same weights over and over again until his muscles finally refused to lift anything lighter than a pencil. He was the apotheosis of happy exhaustion.

The first thing Liz did when they checked into their hotel room was find the power outlet. She was itching to charge up and review her notes from the car trip. She was vaguely aware that she was exhausted, but she was wired too. Brad had no such problems and was asleep the moment his feet landed on the bed and long before his head hit the pillow.

She uploaded the pictures of her new grandchildren and marveled over and over at the little details in the photos. There were tiny moments of adoration, devotion, and love hidden in everyone. She saved them in a new folder marked "Grandbabies," and then got down to the business of the night.

The Jessica Notes were a disorganized stream of consciousness. She had originally started taking the notes to work the experience into a speech. Now they were a collection of anecdotes and reflections, an experience too rich and full to be a simple footnote in a speech. The notes she had taken on the drive, combined with of all the other 'Jessicas' she had known had tipped the collection from "prodigious" to "unwieldy." She set about organizing them, breaking down the behaviors to possible underlying causes. From every angle she looked at it, the answer appeared the same. Lack of self–esteem.

A quick peek at the Internet revealed a number of pre–teen self–esteem programs, a dearth for teen girls, a plethora for college co–eds, and nothing for young professionals.

Liz tried to imagine herself as a young woman again, in her first role of responsibility. How had she handled herself as a woman in a man's world? She was at a loss. She had been so naïve that she did not realize she was outnumbered.

In a flash she realized that while it was a mystery to her, she had not been working in a vacuum. It occurred to her that she could just ask. Liz made a list of all the women she knew as her career had started. It was a small world and she had kept at least somewhat of a track on most of these women. She began making a list of women she knew and women she had worked with and where she thought they might be now.

Liz's fingers froze over the keyboard. The nebulous idea from the treadmill suddenly coalesced, popping solidly into the world like Athena emerging wholly formed from Zeus's head. Her heartbeat sped up and she broke out into a cold sweat.

A brainchild. A passion. A project. The thrill of the chase was on.

This network of women who trail-blazed the way to the board room. The women who originally broke the glass ceiling – these were all women in Liz's peer group. In her network. If she could just harness some of their knowledge, and some of their passion...

Liz labored feverously until deep into the night. Brad roused in the darkness to find Liz illuminated by the light of her computer. He pulled her reluctantly to bed and held her until she finally grew limp and gave herself over to sleep. He knew instinctively that her fallow covalence had finally come to an end, and he slept peacefully.

Note From Robbie:

Giving birth is a great analogy for any project. Creation, particularly innovation, is going to take commitment, effort, and a collision of ideas in new and unexpected ways. An idea can come to you in a flash, but as in Liz's case, it had been nudging her for days. It had been a collection of experiences over a lifetime that prompted her down this new path.

Sometimes creating a business is nine months from conception to execution. For some projects it's an hour of work. Others take a lifetime. If you are considering creating your own business, good for you! Like parenthood, being a business owner can be immensely stressful and incredibly rewarding.

My one solid piece of advice is to FOCUS. You cannot be all things to all people and trying to "hedge" your bets. Don't fall into the trap that if you do multiple things and one fails, you will be okay. This is just false. Focus! Focus! Focus! It's the only way you will achieve ultimate success!

Chapter 17
Conference

Jessica shifted her feet outside the hotel bar. The conference was in full swing, two days down, one half-day plus evening party to go... There was a dull roar of frivolity coming from the bar. The balls of her feet were on fire in her new heels and she wanted desperately to go to her room and collapse into a coma for 12 hours.

"This is what you're here for. This is what you're here for," she chanted to herself in a singsong voice.

The previous night she had ordered room service to her room after the day had wrapped up. Around 11 she bullied herself down to the bar and stood anonymously in a corner observing. After an hour she had retreated back to her room, her TV, her pillow. She had woken up the next morning determined to rock the conference. And she had.

Alan had worn a skinny red tie that had caught her eye the day before. It was very on-trend; his girlfriend must have helped him pick it out. The tie matched her new high heels and purse perfectly. She had rapped on his door a full hour before breakfast was being served.

When he opened the door, bleary eyed and tousled, she was relieved to see that he was alone in the messy room. She wasn't ready for her impression of him to be ruined by some sort of sordid discovery. She had asked if he had a second tie today and then begged for the first one. He had handed it over with an "if you insist" look that only people in long-term relationships can manage.

When breakfast was served an hour later, she had re-imagined herself as the fashionable woman with a tie. The meetings went pretty much the same, her contracted suppliers liked her the same, but the difference was with the rest of the attendees. Suddenly she was noticed. People were asking about her. People wanted to know who she worked for.

Just before lunch one of her target prospective suppliers, a man twice her age and who gleefully showed her pictures of his grandchildren, sought her out and invited her to his table. He confided to her that he had wanted to meet her the first day but couldn't find her. When he had asked after her the second day, he was told to look for the woman with the tie.

Up until that moment she had wondered if she was fetishizing herself. There were a lot of young men at the conference and she had squirmed under the weight of their sudden attention. After the older man, (and the appointment for a serious contract discussion after the conference) the "NOTICE ME!" tie seemed like a savvy business move after all.

Now the bar loomed before her. She had purposefully not changed, meeting a supplier for dinner and then carefully timing her appearance in the bar for shortly after. It would make sense that she was still dressed for business, still wearing a tie, right? She now had a brand and needed to be recognized by it.

Alan appeared by her side and offered his arm. "Tie was a good move. Should I expect you banging on my door at 6AM for another?"

Jessica shook her head. "It was a one-trick pony. I couldn't pull it off with the dress I'm wearing tomorrow."

Alan nodded. "Shall we?" he offered to escort her to the bar.

"We shall." Jessica allowed herself to be guided into the pulsing music and loud voices.

Alan disappeared almost immediately after getting her a drink. He was there one moment and then *blink!* he was swallowed up by the crowd. Jessica sipped and wandered, sipped and wandered... She made some eye contact, exchanged some smiles, and greeted some people she had met over the previous two days. Some offered to buy her drinks and she accepted. It would be rude to decline, right?

She smiled and said "Bye!" to a prospective supplier who was calling it a night when a short man appeared in the void that the prospect had left.

"Are you a lesbian?"

Jessica glanced around in confusion. Yes, he was talking to her. Yes, he was staring at her tie. Or at her breasts beneath the tie. "Um. No?"

The guy let out an overly dramatic sigh of relief. He tilted his head and wiped imaginary sweat off of it, and then righted himself quickly to avoid tipping over. "You are *hot!*"

"Thank you?" She could feel her cheeks were on fire. Did he think she would sleep with him to prove she wasn't a lesbian? She began to frantically scan the room for someone she knew. Anyone.

"Can I buy you a drink?"

"Yes!" *What an excellent idea,* she thought. He joined the crowd around the bar which was three deep with her order (rum and coke) and Jessica determined that she would slip away before he returned.

A quick exploration of the sides of the room revealed lounges and most of her co-workers gathered chatting in a dim corner. She wandered over, *safety in numbers.*

Alan spotted her as she walked up. "There you are!" He was seated on the couch, his posture entirely relaxed. Jessica smiled at his hazy, dopey, happy-to-see you smile and for a moment could glimpse the well-meaning frat boy he had probably been in his college days. "This is good. Have some!" he offered the drink in his hand.

She glanced at her co-workers standing around Alan in a semi-circle. They were all buzzed, but Alan was tipping over the line and into drunk. Her co-workers looked like they would literally heap judgment upon Alan at any moment. She took the proffered drink, ostensibly to keep *him* from drinking any more and gave it a try. Vodka and red bull. *Ew.*

"I'm thirsty. I really need a water," Jessica said pointedly. "Do you want a water too?"

Alan smiled vaguely, "Okay."

Jessica made her way into the mosh pit surrounding the bar. There was only one frantic, overworked bartender on duty. His eyes had gone the glaze of a shell-shocked caged animal... Jessica sipped the taurine drink in her hand rather than have it splash onto her blouse. It tasted like an armpit – not that she had ever tasted an armpit.

By the time she reached the bar she was a jittery, caffeinated buzz teetering towards drunk.

The bartender banged a bell near the cash register and bellowed "Last Call!" before finally making it to Jessica. With two bottled waters in hand, she turned to find Mister Lesbian directly behind her. "There you are!" he crowed. He was holding two drinks, each half full. She tucked a water bottle under one arm and accepted the proffered drink.

"I drank some," he admitted apologetically. "It kept spilling."

She took a sip to clear the taurine taste from her mouth. There was no way she'd be able to get herself another drink before the bar closed. "Thanks." She wondered how she'd be able to shake this guy before heading over to her coworkers. She did not want him to embarrass her. But Alan needed water.

Nope. Mister Lesbian was stuck to her like glue. She mentally shrugged, going back to the safety in numbers idea.

Alan was gone. "Where is he?" she inquired to Charlene.

"He's drunk!" she laughed. "He went to his room. I think." Charlene looked her up and down, plainly wondering how drunk she was, if she would chase after Alan, and throw herself into his bed. Then Charlene's eyes flicked to Mister Lesbian and her body language changed.

"Hi, I'm Charlene," she purred.

Mister Lesbian looked startled. *Two beautiful women!* was stamped on his forehead. "David Gordon, Tronic Systems," he said, holding out his hand.

Oh shit! Jessica recalled the name. From her to-meet list. A prospective supplier. She downed the rest of her drink, frantically trying to remember if she had said anything embarrassing so far. She couldn't remember. Her teeth felt numb–drunk.

She dropped the empty glass and grabbed a card out of her purse to formally introduce herself. David snagged the card and bit the corner, eyeing her up and down salaciously, "You were looking for me, weren't you?"

"For work stuff. Yeah, we could do business together."

"Really? You want to *earn* my business?"

He leaned forward and touched her arm. Charlene looked amused. Jessica pulled away, her skin crawling. She wished she wasn't so drunk. When he touched her again and said, "I have a way to..." Jessica completely surprised herself by yelling, "I'M NOT GOING TO GIVE YOU A BLOWJOB!"

And just like in an awkward comedy movie, the music shut off right as she yelled BLOWJOB. Everyone turned to stare. Jessica could feel her cheeks turning bright red. In the silence, she fled the room.

Note From Robbie:

It can be very challenging to attend a business function where there is lots of free flowing alcohol and not take advantage of the situation. Unfortunately mixing alcohol and business is often a disaster. Everything in moderation is the best motto.

As a good friend recounted of her mistake, "Early in my career there was a company holiday party. I enjoyed myself, had silly conversations, and generally conducted myself as if I was at a close friend's home. As the night grew late, I looked around the room and had a sobering realization. Everyone else was happy, but sober.

"Most people at the party had coke or club soda in their glasses, garnished with some fruit to make it look as if they had alcohol. In fact, for every glass of mixed drink consumed, most had another two with no alcohol at all. I was in the precarious position of having to rewind every conversation I had had that night, trying to recall whether I had embarrassed myself or not."

Bottom line, know your limits and stay well below them. Have drinks with your friends but keep it out of the workplace functions.

Chapter 18

O.P.M.

Liz frowned as she listened to a panicked Jessica on the other side of the line.

"It was like that nightmare where you go to school and you're naked." Jessica concluded miserably.

"Let me get this straight." Liz listed off, "It was a potential supplier. You were having drinks. He said you could get his business if you gave him a sexual favor."

"He implied."

"How clearly did he imply?"

"Pretty clearly. He kept touching me."

Liz was speechless. She NEVER encountered this level of blatant harassment in her days... "And you screamed at him. Did you hit him?"

"No," Jessica responded, "I would never hit someone... but I sure found a part of myself I did not know was in there... The music stopped. You could have heard a pin drop. Everyone was staring and my voice was doing that horrible female shrill thing."

"I think I might have punched him. But I am not sure why you are embarrassed." Liz asked, "What exactly do you think you did wrong?"

"I lost a supplier. I made a fool of myself. I –"

"You were sexually harassed and you held your ground."

"I over reacted."

"No. You didn't." Liz told her in a tone that brooked no argument. "You are so conflict adverse that you are willing to take the blame for this to make it better, to make it go away. You are not comfortable with constructive conflict let alone this craziness."

"I shouldn't have been so drunk."

"That may be true, but that's not relevant right now. Listen to me, Jessica," Liz told her firmly. "You called because you trust my judgment, right?"

"Yes, but–"

"Get your ass downstairs and work the last day of this conference. Do not retreat. Do not acknowledge any event, any blame, anything." Liz continued, letting her voice soften, "Most people weren't there and don't know. Do not put yourself in a place where you are stuck reliving it with every random stranger. Act like you can let it go and keep going. Plus, that guy is so lucky that you did not call security or his boss and file a suit against him... we need to think about next steps with that guy but not now... as I said get downstairs now."

"I can do that?"

Liz could tell that Jessica was almost convinced. "Yeah. We can talk about everything else later, but right now you need to get to that conference... You have to hold your head high and you have work to do."

Jessica agreed, reluctantly. After a few more minutes they rung off and Liz turned back to her coffee date.

"Who was that?" Marie asked, curiously.

"Jessica. A wonderfully smart young woman who is trying to make her way in the corporate world. Unfortunately, she is self-conscious and conflict adverse. So it's a bit of a challenge."

Marie had flown in to meet her new niece and nephew the day before. As her mother's daughter, Marie had held each baby approximately 20 minutes apiece and then was antsy to check her email, go for a walk, get a coffee, anything to get away from the forced calm of the maternity house.

They would go back after coffee and lunch, but for now Marie could use her loud voice and talk with her hands and Liz could catch up with all that was new and interesting with Marie.

"Not to be rude, Mom, but why are you getting involved?"

Liz laughed to herself. Marie had been born with self-assurance and the world had rewarded that every step of the way. She spent the next few minutes explaining the difference between her and women like Jessica, and how much she loved helping her and mentoring her.

"So you're her business shrink." Marie concluded.

"Sure." Liz agreed amiably enough. "Mentor, shrink, career counselor, all the same, right?"

"I could have used someone like you," Marie mused. "When I was starting my business. After watching you for years, I still didn't understand how hard it was."

Liz frowned. She thought Marie's health and wellness app had had a great start. She thought that she'd offered plenty of help, but maybe Marie had needed advice from someone who wasn't her mother. "Are you happy with it?"

"Sometimes. Sometimes I miss having the

corporate paycheck, the assistant to pawn stuff off on. Less responsibility."

"Entrepreneurship isn't for everyone," Liz said carefully.

"OMG, Mom!" Marie gasped. "I'm not quitting my business! I'm allowed to occasionally wish for my corporate benefits package."

Liz laughed in relief. "I was worried for a moment that I had pushed you into a world of entrepreneurship."

"No," Marie bit her lip. Liz suddenly noticed that Marie was tense, her shoulders were almost to her ears. She had both hands wrapped around the coffee cup as if it was a life preserver.

"What is it?" Liz asked... "What's the matter?"

"Well," Marie said carefully, "I think I could use your advice now. My company is suddenly growing quickly and it's," she shook her head, "exciting and stressful and this incredible rollercoaster that I'm barely holding onto."

Liz let out her frozen breath of worry in a *whoosh. This is business!* Liz could have laughed in relief.

Marie, oblivious, was continuing. "We are all very excited BUT the cash flow for this growth isn't balancing in the books. We have to reinvest and grow the infrastructure and the money is going out just as fast as it is coming in... My CFO and I have run the numbers every which way and the bottom line is that we need some investors to fund this growth."

Liz nodded, still awash in relief, but listening closely. Yes. This is something she knew a lot about.

"I don't want investors and all the baggage they bring. I have friends who wish they had never taken outside money and I don't want to be like them... but I don't see any other choice," she held a hand to stop Liz from speaking. "To be clear, I am NOT looking for money from you and Dad. This is not a family problem; this is a company problem. But Mom? I have to solve it in the right way. I could really use your advice."

"You scared the crap out of me," Liz laughed in relief. "I was halfway to convincing myself you had some sort of terminal disease."

"Oh!" Marie said, startled. "Oh, Mom, I would have come to you right away if it was personal, you know that. I'm fine! I just need $5 million dollars." Marie paused, shocked at herself for saying the number out loud, and then she started to laugh... The laughter had a hysterical edge to it and Liz understood.

Oh yes, I remember that feeling. She was tempted to ask to look at the numbers and see if there was something else that could be done, but she knew Marie and she knew her CFO. If Marie said they needed money, they needed money.

"I'm so proud of you," Liz said. "Exponential

growth is amazing and scary and I totally get it. Are you ready to talk strategies? Or do you want to–"

"Yes! Now!" Marie interrupted.

"Ah–ha!" Liz said, one more piece falling into the puzzle. "You didn't just come for the twins."

"Well they're cute, but not so great with the financial advice."

"You are *so* my daughter."

Marie nodded. "Yep. So what do you got?"

Liz snapped her fingers at Marie's purse. "What do you got for me? I assume you brought your research."

Marie slid a folio from her carpetbag of a purse. Inside was some research on a couple of venture capital firms, private equity firms, as well as some serious angel capital funds.

Liz scanned the list, "What kind of due diligence have you done on these firms?"

"Um."

Liz glanced up. "You need to do just as much research on them as they do on you. You are entering into a long–term relationship with these investors. It's like you are starting a family together. You should have the same values as your partner before you jump into bed and make a metaphorical company baby together."

"Baby is already there. I need a baby–daddy."

Liz tried to suppress a chuckle. "Baby daddy needs to get something out of the deal too. This is what I call OPM, Other People's Money."

"Before you take a penny from any of these people, just imagine yourself flying to Europe with them. You're in the middle seat. They are on either side. Just close your eyes and picture the bobbing head and the elbows. If you feel like you could get to Paris with them, sane and with your boundaries intact, I think you'll be fine."

She chuckled, no doubt imagining her potential investors crammed into economy class seats. Marie had a million questions and they talked about the possible terms that might be offered and where Marie could negotiate. It was a good conversation and Liz was glad her daughter could come to her for advice.

Eventually the conversation moved back towards Liz and her business plans.

"So, assuming you don't take Dad's version of retirement, what's next on the agenda for you?"

Liz thought for a moment, trying to figure out how to phrase that nebulous idea that had started materializing a few nights before. "Interesting phenomenon I have been observing over the past few years – when women get to a certain age, they seem to begin to fade. Everything fades, your lips lose their color, your eyebrows almost disappear and of course your hair loses its color... But the worst part – or the most interesting part – is that other people seem to see you differently."

Marie's eyebrows had puckered together slightly. Liz could tell that she was trying to puzzle that out, respecting her enough not to turn a glib joke and move on.

"It's like society wants us to disappear. They want us to retire. They want us to play the TV grandma or the dying matriarch that the young people rally around. It's dismissive. It's a condescending role to force the amazing women of my generation into."

"So you are going into the TV business?"

"No. But there are a lot of women who fought their way into the boardroom who are about to go out to pasture. They'll start volunteering fulltime, or grab a lounge chair on a beach somewhere and leave the game. That is just wrong. My generation pioneered a lot of the women's movement and the movement is encountering a series of setbacks. There has to be a way to harness all that experience, all that fight for the next generation."

"Like Jessica?"

"Maybe." Liz agreed, lost in her own train of thought. "It's an invisible brain trust, you know? My generation fading physically, but intellectually, we know so much. I hate the idea of getting shoved into the traditional 'old lady' box."

"First of all you are not an old lady, Mom, but I get what you're saying." Marie agreed... "As much as I can, anyway. I just don't know how a business could harness all that, so I guess that the white boards are probably already marked up with all of this."

Liz nodded. "It will be once we get home. I think it's probably a non-profit because I cannot figure out a revenue model for it."

Marie grinned. "You realized the irony, don't you?"

"Hmm?"

"You don't want to get shoved into the volunteer box but you are starting a non-profit."

Liz dismissed Marie with a wave and a laugh. They wrapped up and wandered back to the maternity house again. It had been a joke, but late that night Liz couldn't sleep, wondering about age, experience, and giving back.

Note From Robbie:

Working with investors is complicated. You need them but they also need you or someone like you. Understanding what each side brings to the table is VERY important. Do the same level of due diligence on them as they do on you and it usually works out.

If you are faced with raising money, be aware of the good, the bad, and the ugly... Investors are not bad people but their motivation is to achieve a good return on their investment. If they don't want a return, they give their money to charity or a socially-aware cause, but not your company mission statement. You will be expected to always look for a return for your investors.

Be smart about raising money, by raising what you need, not what you'd like to have. Raising too much money often brings more problems than solutions. In fact, when you take someone else's money, you are not working for yourself anymore, you are working for them. How the money is spent must be a benefit for all parties involved. When things are going well it is glorious, and often when things are not going as planned, it can be a nightmare. Do your homework before you take that check.

Chapter 19
Boondoggle

Ken examined Jessica oversteepled fingers. She tried desperately to hold his gaze, hold the need to squirm. She had no idea why she had been called to his office. Was she about to get fired for the conference debacle? It had been an embarrassing moment, yes, but she had landed appointments with every other prospective supplier she had planned to meet. The contracts were practically lining themselves up to be signed. She mentally scrambled to run whatever gauntlet he had in store for her.

"Every year," Ken began slowly, "there is a President's Weekend. It's a where we celebrate and reward the top members of the sales team with golf, tennis, and wine, and so on. This year it's in Scottsdale, Arizona."

Jessica nodded. It was the ritzy part of Phoenix. Her father, a huge baseball fan, made a pilgrimage there every March to watch spring training. She let her shoulders relax a little. Not a "You're FIRED!" conversation after all. Maybe.

Ken continued, "It's really a boondoggle, but is important for the sales people to feel appreciated and recognized for their contribution... We give out awards and slap the credit card down on the open bar. Every year it's the same core group with one or two occasional new players. It's the company's way of boosting those salesy egos."

Jessica frowned. It sounded like Ken really didn't respect the sales people very much. Then again, Ken was condescending to everyone not directly above him in the company food chain.

"One thing that the sales guys want, in addition to all the pats on the back and the perks, is to know what's in the release pipeline for the upcoming year. That way these top sales people are the FIRST to know."

Jessica thought she could see where this was going. She would need to write a presentation for Ken to give at this 'boondoggle.' She adjusted herself in her seat, readying herself to take notes on what he required.

"*You*," Ken emphasized slowly, "will be *giving* two presentations to this group."

Jessica sat stunned and said nothing. A wheel

in her head seemed to be slipping, repeating two ideas as if they were two puzzle pieces that she could worry together into a rational picture. *I'm giving two presentations. I'm going to Arizona? I'm giving two presentations. I'm going to Arizona?* Something finally clicked.

"What about?"

Ken laughed. "Your face is priceless." He shook his head as if to clear the image. "You have one product, but there are two presentations that would add value to the President's Weekend. On the first day you will present the product, building the buzz about the features and benefits of your product line. The next day you'll get into the nitty gritty, providing scenarios of how customers will benefit and the potential Return on Investment. They are going to lose their collective minds."

"Oh my God." Jessica tried frantically to come up with something more intelligent to say. Finally, she blurted out the first thing that popped into her head. "My product is so small!"

"You took on a project that no one wanted." Ken leveled with her. "No one wanted it because it was complicated to implement. Yes, the product line itself is small in scope, but to the sales people, this is the answer to their prayers."

Jessica felt her eyes go wide. She was answering prayers?

"Every year we get requests for this solution. Every year we say 'it's coming.' This year you had the patience and tenacity to get it finally moving through the pipeline. The product line is a lynch pin. It removes barriers and objections, it will drive upgrades and add-ons. These sales people earn most of their money from commissions. They are going to bow down at your feet."

Jessica's mind whirled. Why had no one told her that her project was this important? And underneath all the shock, her mind was already trying to organize presentations.

"No clients present?"

"Nope. This is an internal only."

"And I'm going?"

"Yes," he confirmed.

Jessica nodded to herself.

"Congratulations!" Ken said, shifting papers on his desk and turning towards his computer. She was being dismissed. Jessica stammered a thank you and gathered her things to go. She had the door open and had almost escaped when he added, "Pace yourself at the open bar."

She flushed. So he had heard. Jessica nodded and went back to her desk, her mind a turmoil of excitement, fear, and a tinge of embarrassment...

It wasn't too long before Charlene's head appeared over the side of her cubicle. If Jessica had been sitting in Ken's position during the meeting, she would have seen Charlene mosey casually by and glance in, twice.

"How'd your meeting with Ken go?"

"Have you ever done one of these presentations at the President's Weekend?"

Charlene's eyes narrowed. "You're going?" she demanded.

"Yeah. To talk about the new product line. I don't even know where to begin with the presentation! Have you done one? Or seen one?"

Charlene looked like she had bitten a lemon. "Not really."

Jessica was not sure what "not really" meant other than NO. This wasn't a conference where the whole product team invented reasons to go and the powers-that-be rolled their eyes and said yes on occasion. This was *exclusive*. Invitation only. No gate crashers allowed. Charlene had probably never been.

"Oh," she wished she could think of something clever to say. Something to take the sting away and make Charlene forget she had said anything. How on earth would she ever stand in front of the best people in the company and convince them to be excited?

The awkward moment with Charlene was broken when an email chimed through. It was the retreat details from Ken. Her eyes were pulled to the screen, devouring every word. Charlene quietly disappeared.

"Crap!" Jessica said when she discovered that the first draft of both presentations was due in 30 days. She hit the forward button and sent the email to Liz, changing the RE: to HELP!

After clicking the refresh button on her email obsessively for five minutes straight, Jessica stood up to go find Alan. Liz might not be in her office. She needed to move her antsy, anxiety filled body.

"Congrats," Alan said when he saw her. News had already spread. "That's pretty exciting!"

"I had no idea my product was important," Jessica admitted. She hoped she didn't sound like she was bragging, but she couldn't hide her feelings. "I'm going to be a wreck, just wait and see."

After a little chit-chat, Jessica was able to determine that Alan had also never been invited to a President's Weekend. He had no idea what the presentation should look like either. He imagined it to be like an Apple "big reveal" press conference and Jessica felt herself pale. When she finally made it back to her desk, Liz's email was waiting.

Jessica,

This is very exciting and very scary, I know, but you will do very well...but before we dig into your presentation I need to tell you that it is really not very cool to forward an internal email to an external person. I know you feel very comfortable with me but there were a few items in that email string you forwarded that were confidential or close to confidential. Next time cut and paste the meat of the issue into an email and send it my way or to someone else. Or a phone call would work too. It keeps things clean and simple.

Okay, now to the fun stuff... your presentation! Before we actually create the presentation I want you to pretend that you have already launched this new product line and you and some of your colleagues are doing a talk show. I have attached a visual for you to use as you imagine how you might answer the questions. Write down your answers, practice talking about them, and then let's get together and role play. Don't freak out – it's fun and it will just be the two of us. I will help you. Since you only have 30 days until the first draft, let me know how soon you have time to do this. I come back from LA (grandbabies!) day after tomorrow and I'll make my schedule work for you.

If you are wondering why I am asking you to do this strange exercise which does not make actual progress on your presentation, please just trust me that it will make a big difference. COOL?

See you soon.

Liz

Attached to the email was an illustration.

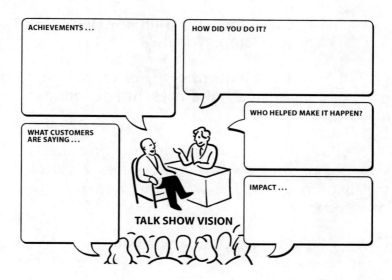

Note From Robbie:

Most companies have privacy policies and confidentiality agreements. Navigating these appropriately with your mentor is important. While you may feel comfortable disclosing information to your mentor, it doesn't mean that your employer is comfortable with it, or that by disclosing company information that you aren't putting your mentor in a bad position.

Before hitting forward on an email to your mentor – or anyone outside of the company, for that matter – consider:

1. Are you exposing confidential or proprietary information?

2. Are you disclosing email addresses and contacts that should not be public information?

3. Are you breaking company rules or terms of your employment?

4. Will the information make your mentor an "insider" and present her with a moral dilemma?

If you forward any email, the information is now out of your control and can be re-forwarded to anyone, anywhere. Are you prepared for the consequences?

When forwarding company email, think twice or three times before you do. Always use your best judgment.

Chapter 20

Change is Good

The double stroller was roughly three people wide and took up the entire sidewalk. The twins inside were still immobile and tiny in comparison to the vast carriage built to ferry them through the next few years. Liz walked a pace back from Ashley, as she hefted the ungainly contraption down the street. The combined weight of the kids would be roughly 80 pounds before the stroller would be retired. Liz felt a stab of pity for Ashley.

Marie chatted amiably next to Liz, but loud enough that Ashley would hear. They were making the half-mile pilgrimage to the beach. It would be the twins' first exposure to the beach, the ocean, the thing that made living in southern California so desirable and so expensive. It was also Liz's last day before going home. It had been two glorious weeks.

Liz was antsy to get back to her life. Not only was the literacy project waiting patiently in the wings, she was also excited to start adding her thoughts on The Invisible Brain Trust to her whiteboard.

They made their way down the boardwalk, window shopping, enjoying the fresh air. It was a little crowded and Ashley struggled to navigate the traffic.

"Liz?"

Liz started, turned. A middle aged man, a little taller than herself was looking at her curiously. He looked vaguely familiar but she couldn't place him.

"Sam? From Ace, Inc.? Oh, 20 years ago?"

"Oh my goodness, Sam! How are you?" she opened her arms and hugged him. He was older, had lost some hair, but had also lost some of the pudginess she remembered of him. He looked healthy, sun-kissed and when they hugged, she could feel strength in his arms.

"You look really good," she said when they parted.

"You too!" he smiled warmly. "Let me introduce you to my family." He coaxed forward his partner and an awkward teenage boy who wanted to be anywhere other than hanging out on a pier with his two dads.

"John, Aaron, this is the woman who encouraged me to leave Ace, Inc. Without her I would have never met you," he squeezed John's shoulder, "or you, for that matter," he told Aaron. Aaron flushed.

"So nice to meet you," Liz shook John's hand with genuine warmth. Sam had not been "out" 20 years ago, but in retrospect, it made sense. She had known an overweight, frustrated young man. Before her was a confident, healthy, happy adult.

Liz introduced Ashley and Marie, and proudly displayed the grandtwins, as she was beginning to think of them. She noted that this was the first time she was able to show off her grandkids and even though she was tired of being in Southern California, she would miss them.

Sam, as it turned out, was on the forefront of the apps business when the iPhone was introduced. He was a very happy, comfortable man now. When they parted a few minutes later, they exchanged business cards and a promise to catch up the next time she was in town. Liz was grinning ear-to-ear as her entourage pulled her down the pier.

"Until I saw his partner, I thought maybe the two of you had a little sumpin' sumpin' back in the day." Marie teased.

Ashley and Liz both laughed. "When he worked for me, he was the unhappiest tech support guy on the face of the planet. Just miserable."

Liz caught an incredulous look between Marie and Ashley. "What did you do?"

She smiled, "I fired him."

"What?!" Marie exclaimed. "You fired him and he just worshipped you in public?"

"It wasn't a mean, **YOU'RE FIRED!** kind of thing. I tried to coach him for close to a year. He was obviously smart, but unhappy. He'd come in hungover, drag out his deadlines, self-sabotage his projects. When I let him go, I encouraged him to do something that mattered to him. Apparently he found it."

Liz was suddenly reminded of Jessica. As far as she knew, Jessica was straight, but definitely unhappy, self-sabotaging, and truly afraid of getting fired. She wondered if maybe a firing would be the best thing for her. So Jessica would be free to chase whatever would ultimately make her happy. Of course, she would never be able to say that out loud to Jessica, but maybe surviving her "worst nightmare" would build some self-confidence.

"Have either of you ever been fired?"

Ashley and Marie both squirmed uncomfortably. "I'll take the fifth." Marie said.

"Ditto." Ashley agreed.

"Really!" Liz felt her eyebrows hit her hairline. Not that she thought being fired was all that terrible, but being discreet was out of character for Marie. Marie tended to over share – much to her father's chagrin, she had come home from her first semester in college and announced she was on the pill.

"Well whatever happened, I hope you took a lesson from it."

"I don't think I'll be hugging a former boss anytime soon," Marie laughed, "but I am happier now than I was then."

Ashley adjusted the blankets covering the twins. "My path led me to these two. I've got no regrets."

Ashley was the very picture of exhausted happiness and Liz 100% believed her. She also offered to push the stroller on the way back...

Note From Robbie:

I think everyone I've ever fired, I've seen again. It's a small world and most industries are even smaller. With that in mind, it's important to handle hiring, firing, and quitting in a professional manner.

Everyone is on their best behavior during the interview process. But until you start working together it's hard to know if an employee/employer relationship is really going to work. If the job isn't clicking, or the company culture isn't for you, that's okay. Most employers would rather you bow-out early than to invest time and money coaching someone who is clearly miserable.

The key is to take your leave in a professional manner. Leverage an introduction to a potential new employer. Get a recommendation from your direct supervisor. Give an appropriate amount of notice. As tempting as it is, avoid making the grand display and huffing your distain on your way out the door.

It's important to also note, that if you have been fired in the past, you are not branded with a Scarlett Letter for life. Being fired doesn't change who you are, it just means that that particular job, with that particular company was not a good fit. Dust yourself off and get back out there.

Chapter 21
Talk Show

Jessica waited anxiously for Liz to arrive. She was on the patio of the café she'd taken Liz to after her bender with Sarah. *The hangover café,* as she thought of it. It was unusual for Jessica to get there first and she wondered nervously if she had misunderstood where Liz had asked to meet her.

As she leaned down to retrieve her phone from her purse, to re-check the location and time, she spotted the "talk show" worksheet folded neatly in the side pocket. She pulled it out with her phone and checked it over one last time.

It wasn't supposed to be hard, Jessica understood that much. But what was it supposed to look like when it was completed? She had considered getting someone's opinion in the Cube Farm (she had been moved this week to a cube with a view – fancy pants compared to the gloom of the Cubby Hole) but she didn't want anyone to know she had a mentor. Instead, she had guessed wildly, convinced she was doing the exercise all wrong.

Jessica confirmed the location and time, then settled in to wait, re-reading her answers to pass the time.

Achievements: *My company had a very successful product line for many years but over time customers began asking for a few new features that would keep them from having to switch to a competitor. The cost of change in my business is very high for the customer so I think we got a bit complacent. The sales team was really beating the drum on some features and the combination finally got senior management's attention. They allocated resources to add these new features. I volunteered to manage the launch of this new product line before I knew it was so critical and in such demand. It was very scary at times but we focused and we stuck to the timeline, even though it meant many long nights and weekends. We knew testing and quality assurance were really key, to be a seamless solution to fit into our existing product line and infrastructure. Our hard work paid off. We launched the product with our new feature on time and on budget. It was so much work but so rewarding to see it happen.*

How did you do it? *When I took on this project I had no idea what to do but I knew that I worked best when I was part of a team that had great* *communication, a clear and open project plan, and a person or two to handle problems calmly - so that is what I tried to create. I was not completely successful, I had a few meltdowns along the way (I think we all did), but we pulled together and got it done in the end. There was almost no finger pointing or blaming or excuses. It was exhilarating.*

What customers are saying? *The feedback from the customers is great. It is exactly what they wanted - but now they want more! I had no idea that giving them what they wanted would lead to a long list of new features/complaints about what they don't have yet. Senior management had a lot of forethought in this regard – they purposely delayed the new product lines until they could afford to create not only this one piece my team put together but also a pipeline of other improvements which will roll out in the next year. Bottom line is that the existing customers love it and the new customers are signing on in greater numbers than projected.*

Impact…*Well, the impact for me was experiencing the highs and lows of managing a project from conception through launch and the highs of seeing the fruits of my labor praised inside and outside of the team and company.*

The team had to struggle with balancing family and getting this project done, and in some cases it took its toll on relationships. I hated to see that happen but I guess it's the nature of the beast.

The company has now expanded into some new vertical channels that they could not handle before, so revenue is up BUT the costs of rolling out all the new features before our competitors is a juggling act that is not fun.

It was so *weird* to talk about this project as if it was already done, launched, and successful. A flash of movement caught her eye and she looked up in time to see Liz approaching with her arms open. Jessica stood to exchange hugs and pleasantries.

"I'm so sorry I'm late," Liz explained. "We only got back yesterday and it's been crazy trying to get back in the routine! Laundry, settling back into my office, and oh my God I must be getting old – I've never been so happy to sleep in my own bed! I've been white boarding a business idea all morning too. I'm glad we scheduled this or I probably wouldn't leave my office at all today!"

"White boarding?" Jessica asked, smiling. Liz seemed positively full of non–stop energy.

"Yeah! I have white boards all over my office walls. I've got a lifetime supply of dry erase markers too. I'll show you sometime. But ANYWAY! Down to business. Did you complete the Talk Show exercise?"

Jessica felt a twinge of disappointment and embarrassment. She wanted to hear about Liz's trip, see pictures of the twins, and NOT show her the dismal attempt at the talk show prompts. "Nope." She held Liz's gaze while slowly refolding the paper and trying to slip it back into her purse unnoticed.

Liz laughed and held out her hand. "Nice try."

Jessica slid the folded paper over reluctantly. "I think I did it wrong."

Liz glanced at the answers scribbled in the bubbles and smiled. "There is no right or wrong way to do this. So... we are going to act out this talk show. You ready?"

"Seriously?" Jessica tried to stall. This was bizarre.

"Seriously," Liz replied before launching into her best Oprah impression. "Jessica!

Thanks so much for coming by to chat with me! Please tell everyone about what you have accomplished this year at XYZ Company."

Jessica could feel her glasses shift as her eyebrows compressed into a skeptical quirk. She reached out for her paper so she could read her lines, but Liz held the paper aloft, out of her reach.

"No need to read."

Jessica looked at her incredulously and then shifted uncomfortably in her seat. For the first time Jessica felt truly unsure of Liz. Like maybe she was about to see the tougher side of Liz that she knew was there but had never experienced...

Liz seemed to catch some of that feeling in the air and touched Jessica's hand. "It's just roleplaying. Just us."

Jessica nodded slowly. *Just Liz. She's safe. Trust a little longer.* Liz hummed a few bars, smiling. Jessica realized it was the first few notes of "Raindrops on Roses" and suddenly understood that she had stopped breathing. *Subtle Liz.*

Liz repeated her prompt and this time Jessica breathed and replied. "My company had a very successful product line but it was dated and customers were switching to competitors. The sales team was asking for a specific feature that was in-demand for their clients. I volunteered to manage the launch of this feature and after a lot of work, testing, and sleepless nights, it launched on time and on budget. It was so much work, but so rewarding to see it happen."

Jessica noted that her voice had cracked here and there and that she had skipped over whole sentences that were written down in the corresponding bubble. But it felt like the natural way to answer the question verbally. Liz was nodding and asked the next question.

The interview bantered back and forth with Liz asking questions and teasing out information and Jessica growing more at ease with this "talk show" format. Jessica noted that her shoulders were relaxing and her voice was growing steadier. Her brain was no longer spinning frantically to remember the exact words on the paper, but easily finding natural ways to retell the written answers.

It felt like a natural conversation when Liz concluded with an Oprah style, "Thank you for coming today, Jessica. It's been a real honor." Then Liz dropped character, smiled broadly and then gave her a golf clap.

"Great job my dear, great job! You really gave this assignment some thought and put yourself out there. I am very impressed – and so excited for you!"

Jessica felt pulled up short. The interview experience was cute, but how did exactly did that translate to a presentation?

"I'm a little confused," she said carefully. "That was an interesting exercise and all, but I'm supposed to give a presentation, not an interview." She hoped like hell that this was a tactful enough approach.

"Oh yes. I know."

The silence spun out.

"My presentation is due in three weeks," Jessica explained slowly, trying to fight back a wave of panic that was threatening to overtake her.

Liz smiled. "Think about what you just did and how comfortable you were talking about the product, your team, the good, the bad, and the ugly. You have a solid story and perspective to describe your thoughts and feelings about this product and the experience of creating it." Liz shifted in her seat, looking for the right words to explain... "Do you get how having a narrative is going to help you create a presentation?"

Jessica wasn't sure and said as much.

"I know!" Liz whipped under the table and

reemerged with a portable whiteboard and two dry erase markers.

"You carry them with you?" Jessica asked incredulously.

"I like them," Liz said shoving the board and markers over the table to Jessica. "You're going to need 10–15 slides right? I'm going to go grab some treats. While I'm gone, write down everything you want people to know when they leave your presentation in Arizona."

Jessica sat staring at the blank white board and colorful markers and took a deep breath. An idea popped into her head and she uncapped the dry erase marker and wrote it down. She wrote down the next thought as well. By the time Liz returned with fresh chocolate chip cookies she had filled the portable white board with ideas (some crossed out and some circled) and began to transfer the best ideas to the back of the Talk Show worksheet.

They ate cookies, Jessica occasionally interrupting the silence with questions or thoughts. Liz discussed the ideas and suggested changes and by the time they were done, Jessica knew she could do this and she could do it well.

"Pro tip?" Liz offered as they began to wrap up the session.

"Hit me with it."

"Take a picture of that whiteboard. You might

find something you need there that you didn't transfer to the rest of your notes."

"Good call." She hugged Liz tightly before they left the café. "Thank you," Jessica whispered.

"You've got this," Liz said giving her a tight squeeze. "I can't wait to see what happens next."

Note From Robbie:

The Talk Show was born into this format after years of coaching startups and trying to get them to visualize and talk succinctly and intelligently about their business! The Talk Show is a great tool to get out of your own perspective and look at the project as it will be when it is completed.

This is just one example of how you can approach a problem from a different perspective... Who hasn't had a daydream of telling their idol all about their work and their passion? Or having a documentary or viral video of your work? Taking a step back to create these sort of macro-views of your work can help tell your story, and clarify your end goals.

Why is telling your story important? Well, it is a way to express your mission, your company culture, your reason for putting the hours of your life into your work. It is a way to attract the right talent to your cause and push your agenda forward. It is how you will open your work to new solutions and breakthroughs. It provides the confidence for your elevator pitch, your customer pitch, your investor pitch, and more.

Never underestimate the importance of seeing your work from all sides. Give yourself room to maintain scope and objectivity. Your work and your business will only thrive as a result.

Chapter 22
The Fight

Liz finally felt like she could breathe again. The first few days back from Evan and Ashley's, she had been overwhelmed by her neglected life. The email had been managed, but nothing else in her office had been touched. She was so grateful for her housekeeper for keeping the house tidy, laundry done, and tossing the spoiled food in the fridge... Her life would be completely unmanageable without her.

Now the Invisible Brain Trust notes were up on the whiteboards and competing for space with the literacy project... Liz bit her lip in thought as she stood back, examining her handiwork. Brad had not been pleased with her setting up one non-profit, and now it appeared there would be a second.

Hmmm. Speaking of... Liz sniffed the air but

didn't detect dinner in the kitchen. She dug through the papers on her desk and unearthed her phone. Brad had beaten her to the punch.

We're celebrating tonight. Reservations at Romanov's at 7:30.

Liz checked the time, smiling. Perfect. She had just enough time to get ready. *But what were they celebrating?* She decided it didn't really matter. Any excuse having a good dinner, good wine, and good company.

Brad had come home at 6:30 and was scurrying about the house with excitement. Liz had no idea what was going on, she hadn't see him this excited since Evan's call that they would be grandparents. She asked for him to just tell her what was up, but the man loved his surprises (as did she), and she rolled her eyes good-naturedly when he told her to wait and see.

Romanov's was exquisite as always. The dim lights, the twinkling candles on the table, the smell of gourmet food wafting from the kitchens. Her mouth watered looking at the menu. She hadn't realized how hungry she was. She wanted to order the entire menu!

"I'm ordering appetizers," Liz announced.

"Go for it. I'm ordering champagne."

"Mm," she murmured appreciatively. It was going to be one of *those* kinds of nights.

Once the waiter appeared and made his recommendations, they placed their orders and the champagne came first. Brad held up his glass to toast her. "Several toasts tonight. The first, to my lovely wife, mother of my children, and grandmother to two beautiful babies."

Liz smiled and sipped, relishing the bubbles. "Do I have to wait for dinner, or can you tell me the surprise now?"

Brad grinned, reaching into the inside pocket of his jacket and unfolding the square of paper he retrieved... It was a picture of an old house, with SOLD stamped in red letters at the top... Liz stared at the paper dumbstruck.

"The second toast is to our... new home."

She looked up and saw that he was dead serious. And proud... She felt her eyebrows contract into one solid entity. "You bought a house?" She knew it was a dumb thing to say but it just didn't compute.

She struggled with what to say. Brad's proud smile was plastered on his face, but his eyes were getting worried. She finally said, a little louder than she intended, "Are you serious? We can't afford a second home!"

"I haven't even told you about it yet," Brad said quietly, letting his smile go. "I found this amazing house and it's the house we always hoped we would find one day. It was built in 1906 and it's been completely renovated. We always dreamed of owning a vintage home and this one is impeccable."

"And where is this dream home?" Liz hissed, already knowing the answer.

"Santa Monica."

She nodded slowly, "I am very confused. You know that I hate LA, and we have our own life here. The kids have their own lives there. And...in case you forgot from all the other conversations we've had. **I'm not ready to retire!**" Her voice had grown louder, pitching up an octave that she hated hearing herself achieve.

Brad's face had grown sad and stony. "I heard you loud and clear but what about me? More importantly what about us? Does my opinion count or is it only yours that matters?" He was folding the paper and refolding it into tight little squares. "*I* told you I want to retire. *I* told you I want to enjoy being a grandfather. *I* want *us* to live in our dream home."

"Whether I want to or not?" Liz leaned forward towards Brad. "You bought a house without discussing it with me. Do you not see the problem with that?"

"It's our *dream* house!"

"My dream does *not* include living in LA!"

"My dream doesn't include a wife who still works 80 hours a week."

Liz drew back. How could she even reply to that? She got up and quietly left the table, the champagne, and the love of her life. She checked with her inner voice and it nodded in agreement, yes, they were taking the car. Let Brad get an Uber.

She drove three miles to a hotel she had once been to for a conference and parked. Liz sat unmoving behind the wheel, her fingers still gripping the steering wheel as if she were trying to throttle it. Go in? Or go home? She had so many emotions she did not know how to begin to sort them out.

He had bought a house. He *never* did rash or impractical things. She was the impractical one – she was the dreamer. She had to admit it looked like it was their dream house BUT located in one of the most nightmarish places she could imagine. Too close to the kids. Too congested. She tried to envision them in LA but she just could not make it happen. It was completely ungrateful, but she didn't want it. She didn't want anything to do with it...

And, Brad accused me of working 80 hours a week like it was something new! It was so hard to dissect everything wrong with that statement. She worked hard, she put in long hours, but that was true for their *entire* marriage. It felt like he basically said he didn't like who she was and what made her happy. Liz felt tears stinging the back of her eyes and a moment later they were spilling over onto her cheeks. On top of that was a wave of anger... *what was he trying to tell her?*

These two thoughts warred back and forth in her mind, chasing each other in useless, painful circles. As they did, her subconscious chimed in with its own background music, *"It's alright to cry, crying gets the sad out of you, it's alright to cry, it might make you feel better."* The moment she realized she was humming along to the Marlo Thomas tune, her thoughts final broke their cycle and drifted to Marie. Liz used to play that song to Marie when she cried. That was so long ago.

She sighed and resigned herself to a night of loneliness. Deciding to check into the hotel, Liz gathered her things and noticed her phone glowing in her purse. There were about 50 missed calls and text messages from Brad. With a pang of guilt, Liz realized that she had left the restaurant almost three hours ago.

The very last text from Brad was, "WATERMELON!!!" Liz smiled, despite everything. Ages ago, after their first real knockdown-drag-out fight, they had made a solemn pact to never go to bed angry. They had agreed they would stay up and figure it out -even if it took all night and a few times it had.

Watermelon was their safe word – a reminder of that pact. It was something silly to break the tension, to shift the conversation to something more productive. And who could stay angry at the thought of a cold watermelon slice on a summer afternoon? No one.

Liz sent a quick text to let Brad know she was on her way home. She chuckled to herself as she did. If she died on her way home, all the police would know is that there had been a fight with her husband that ended with the cryptic text "WATERMELON!!!"

When Liz pulled into the driveway, all the lights in the house were on and it looked warm and familiar. She took a few deep breaths, adjusting the rearview mirror to examine her reflection. Her eyes were red and puffy. There wasn't much to do about it, but hastily removed the black smudges of makeup anyway.

Inside Brad was sitting on the couch, tensely anticipating her arrival. He sat forward with his hands entwined and dangling between his knees. He looked relieved to see her and nervous, his eyes flicking over her body, trying to get a sense for how this would go.

Liz halted in the doorway and sighed. Part of her really wanted to retreat to her bed and bury herself beneath the comforter. Brad seemed to sense her thoughts because he met her eyes and softly said, "Watermelon."

"Watermelon," she agreed.

Brad stood up and crossed the room to hug Liz. She let him envelop her and she hugged him back, inhaling deeply and smelling his scent, letting the tightness in her shoulders relax. She loved him. They could work through this.

"I'll go first," Liz said when the hug finally broke. "No interrupting, please."

Brad nodded, holding her hand and leading her

back to the couch where they could sit together and talk. Liz noticed that even once they were seated, Brad didn't let go of her hand, as if she might disappear the moment he stopped touching her.

"Our philosophy – what we built our relationship on – is Trust, Respect, Love and a Sense of Humor. It has been our secret recipe for our healthy, happy relationship. But tonight I felt like we didn't have either Trust or Respect. I felt like it was a violation of my trust that you made such a large decision without me. And I felt – and still feel – disrespected that you made such a unilateral decision to move our lives, as if my life, my business, was just a trinket to be packed into a box."

Brad squeezed her hand supportively. Liz had fought the quaver in her voice, but found she needed to take a couple deep breaths to continue.

"You've never done anything like this before, so I feel like I'm missing a huge piece of the puzzle... I need you to please tell me the story of this house and how you came to the decision to buy it without me."

Brad inhaled and chose his words slowly and carefully. "My first marriage was falling apart when Evan was young. When I think about Marie, it was like I blinked and she was in school – I worked myself to death when Marie was little too. When the twins were born, I realized how much I missed when I was a father. How much I wanted to see these little people grow."

He squeezed her hand. "I don't want to be a dad again. But I could be a good grandfather. I don't know if you remember, but Marie was afraid of my dad. He was a stranger to her. He came swooping in with gifts and expecting hugs and to her he was just this stranger.

"I don't want to be a stranger to Liliana and Patrick. I want my grandkids to see me, to recognize me, to be excited that Grandpa is coming over."

He hesitated and this time Liz squeezed Brad's hand encouragingly. He nodded. "This next part sounds like I'm blaming you, but I'm not." He used his free hand to pat their entwined fingers and met her eyes briefly before flicking them away to examine his memories again.

"After the twins were born, I was bored. There was only so much time we could spend with the kids and you were working. I started to look at houses and imagine a retired life down there. At first it was casual, just checking in the paper. There was a lot of crap housing, suburbia stuff, but I ran across this great little area of homes that were preserved from the turn of the century. Walking through that neighborhood is like stepping back in time. It just really caught my imagination.

"There was an open house and I went in and, Liz, the house was horrible. You could tell that they had tried to put the best face on it to sell, but there hadn't been new carpet or a paintbrush in at least 30 years. It was like looking at the perfect apple on the outside that was spoiled on the inside.

"I knew I would never buy it, but I was bored. So I started talking to the real estate agent. She was very nice and completely understood that this house was a fixer–upper - not my cup of tea. She filled me in a bit on the history of the neighborhood and that most of the houses that come up for sale have multiple offers in less than 24 hours.

"I gave her my contact details and told her to call if a renovated house came up in that neighborhood. I wasn't planning on buying – I just really wanted to see what a renovated house would look like. It had caught my imagination that it would be like a finished piece of art."

Brad shook his head, as if clearing away some cobwebs. He looked up, smiling ruefully. "She called the day we were leaving to come back here. I ran over to take a quick peek. I still wasn't planning on buying, I just wanted to see a house living up to its architecture... And Liz. It was amazing." A new energy filled Brad's voice, his eyes glowed with enthusiasm. "It *is* amazing. It is the dream home we talked about years ago. The place where we wanted to live out the golden years of our lives.

"I dreamt about it that night and called the lady back and made an offer the next morning. I didn't think I would get it, but I would never be able to live with myself if I didn't try. And I got it." There was a hint of wonder in his voice. As if he could not believe that this precious thing could exist, never mind belong to him...

"I should have consulted you." Brad apologized, pulling himself back from the mental picture of this dream home. "I got carried away and I blindsided you under the guise of surprising you. You've always loved surprises... until now, I guess." Liz smiled and squeezed his hand. Brad said, "I'm so very sorry. I can cancel the contract and forfeit the deposit." His voice sounded strained at this last bit, as if the idea of letting go of the house was physically painful.

Liz nodded. The first piece of the puzzle had fallen into place. This hadn't been a deliberate decision. It had been a riptide of events, pulling him into deep water before he realized the danger.

"Okay, let's put the house aside for a minute. I understand how we got there and that's something we can work through." Liz gestured with her free hand pushing the invisible house to the side. "There was another piece of our conversation that we still need to talk through, and when it comes down to it, it's more important than a house."

Brad stared at her blankly. "Eighty hours a week," she reminded him.

His eyes went wide and his mouth opened with a dawning horror. "I'm so sorry!" he blurted.

"We can't sweep it under the rug. We've gotta talk about it."

Brad closed his mouth and nodded.

It was midnight before they were done talking. Brad loved her, even though she worked 80 hours a week. She loved Brad, even though he had impulse-bought a house 300 miles away. Before turning in, they logged online and booked roundtrip flights for two to LA. Liz wanted to see the magical house that had caused so much trouble before any final decisions were made.

Note From Robbie:

In this chapter, Liz states that her relationship with Brad is built on Trust, Respect, Love, and a Sense of Humor. These values are the foundation of their marriage. Agreed upon values are incredibly important for the overall success of your partnerships – whether romantic or not.

Of all the values that you can have in a relationship, I believe the most important is Respect. Respect is the keystone that the rest of your foundations are built upon. If you can't respect your partner, your boss or your colleague, you will never trust them, never feel secure in their abilities and will ultimately stress yourself out over the shortcomings of the relationship. If you are in a situation where you don't respect the people you work with, it is time to take steps to move on.

Trust is just as important because you need to be able to depend on your team. You need to believe in their integrity and/or commitment to your goals and projects. If you can't trust your team, you will spend an enormous amount of time second-guessing and double-checking everyone else's work. That's wasteful of your talents and time, as well as theirs!

Chapter 23
Blindspots

Jessica stood in awe, gaping at the whiteboards in Liz's office... They were a riot of color, bullet points, notes, doodles, and arrows. When Liz had told her that there were whiteboards on her walls, Jessica had imagined each wall with a classroom-style framed space on each wall. She had never expected actual floor-to-ceiling whiteboards. Or the notes!

She must use a step ladder! Jessica thought, craning her head up to squint at the project title near the top of the office window. *Invisible Brain Trust.* There was one on the opposite wall titled *Literacy Project.* The wall between the two held a series of interlocking boxes with tiny printed notes and arrows. It looked vaguely familiar to Jessica, but she couldn't place it.

"Grab a pen and write on my walls!" Liz laughed from the doorway. She held two glasses of water and offered one to Jessica.

"I don't really think I'm going to contribute much to the brainstorming, Liz." Jessica looked again in wonder at all the notes on the walls. "It seems like you've thought of everything."

"Mm," Liz murmured. "I haven't. Did you know that every eye has a blind spot? If you close your left eye, and I placed my finger in just the right place, to you it would disappear. Your left eye compensates for the blind spot in the right eye. The right eye compensates for the left eye."

Jessica nodded, appraising the walls again. "I'm here to expose the blind spots."

"Exactly. Plus, collaboration and synergy are key to any project."

Jessica smiled and quirked an eyebrow, "Not just buzz words? Woah –" she interrupted herself. "These statistics are real?" She gestured to the reading stats on the literacy wall.

"Unfortunately. There's some stats on the IBT wall too."

Jessica turned, scanning for the points Liz had indicated, "Holy crap."

- Women are paid 77% of what a man does for the same job.

- Less than 1/3 of young business women are offered any sort of formal mentorship program.

- Women represent 40% of the global workforce but hold less than 15% of corporate executive positions.

Her eyes flicked over the number 77% again. Her chest was clenching. An additional 23% of income and she wouldn't need a roommate. *I need to be paid more.*

She must have said something to that effect, though Jessica didn't remember saying it out loud.

"I'm sure you do. You have worked hard and deserve a raise. Until this retreat is over and your project is launched, your negotiating position isn't the greatest. We'll come up with a strategy after we toast your successful launch."

Jessica nodded mechanically, her eyes fixed on 77%. The shock was starting to wear off, a thought jumped into her mind, waving like a red flag in front of a bull. *Why should I have to prove myself to get paid what a man would get for the same job?*

She struggled to phrase her question to sound less like an accusation. "How do they get away with this?" she finally managed.

"For whatever mysterious reason, women are not the best negotiators for themselves," Liz said simply.

Jessica sighed. She sat heavily into a plush chair in the corner. Understanding dawned on Liz's face. "You didn't negotiate, did you?"

Jessica shook her head.

"It's okay," Liz tried to reassure her. "Almost no women your age do. For some reason women assume that this is what the position pays and you take it or leave it. Men assume that they are supposed to assert themselves and ask for more money before they ever agree to take the job – and they keep asking for raises after that too."

Jessica felt confused. There were rules to the game and she did not know them. She suddenly remembered a guy in her upper level sociology class bragging that he had gotten an A by demanding it during office hours. She had resented him then and hated the entire system now. Guys like that who did half the work and demanded the most were out-earning her in the present and kicking up their feet up in the executive suite ten years from now.

"Are you okay?" Liz asked.

"Where does Human Resources fit in this picture?" Jessica asked bitterly. "Don't they have an obligation to have equal pay for equal roles regardless of gender?"

"In a perfect world, that would be what happens. But in real life, it's not that simple. Experience for example, isn't black and white when it comes to deciding pay. In addition, senior management usually sets a pay scale and then HR monitors it."

Liz shrugged. "I'm not saying it's right, I'm just saying how it is.

"Come on," Liz pulled her out of the chair and positioning her in front of a wall of notes. "I still need your hand with this."

Jessica nodded, trying to refocus on the problem at hand. "Want to give me a primer on all of this?"

"As women age over 60, they undergo this physical transformation," Liz gestured toward her head. "Their hair grows gray or white, their body shape changes, and even their eyebrows and lips fade. The aging process fades women until they are virtually invisible. The natural fading that comes with age has an unfortunate side effect of forcing women to fade into the woodwork of life. All of that is to be expected and we have lots of makeup companies and plastic surgeons lined up to help with that.

"But! Coupled with the physical changes, comes the societal changes. Older women are often seen as philanthropists, grandmothers, bingo players, shoppers, or volunteers, but not often as viable businesswomen... Since I let my dye-job go, no one ever asks me what I do anymore. They ask when I *retired*.

"I got to thinking, why is that? The answer was really quite simple. This, right now, is the first generation of women to have a played a significant senior role in the work force. This is the groundbreaking generation of VPs, consultants, professors, lawyers, and doctors. Now, these same trail-blazing women are being put out to pasture. Some have retired by choice and others have been forced out of the limelight. As hard as they may try, they are perceived as passé, old school, or not relevant any more.

"For the most part, male professionals do not suffer from the very same issues. Men go gray or bald, their body shape changes, their eyebrows get wiry and long, but that is considered okay. We are all accustomed to older, powerful men aging. But we are not accustomed to older, powerful women aging. Make sense?"

Jessica nodded, wondering where this was going.

"So we have this large posse of brilliant and successful women," Liz gestured to an imaginary group to her left, "whose talent and expertise is going to pasture." She shifted her gesture to the right side. "We also have an up-and-coming generation of hard driving glass-ceiling breakers who find themselves in circumstances similar to 50 years ago. They fight a backlash against feminism, equal pay, and rights to control their own reproduction.

"It's history repeating itself, but this next generation doesn't need to reinvent the wheel."

Jessica considered. "There is a brain trust of women who already fought this battle."

"Exactly," Liz agreed. "As I envision it, the Invisible Brain Trust will be a national organization of smart, savvy, successful businesswomen over 60, who have the desire and drive to share their secrets to success... These women do not want to see the progress of feminism and equal rights to be relegated to a footnote in their generational history. The members of IBT will commit to mentoring and cultivating the future businesswomen, entrepreneurs, and thought leaders of the next generation."

Jessica felt a jolt when Liz said 'mentoring.' Was this the outcome Liz had gotten out of mentoring her? Was the experience of mentoring Jessica something that Liz wanted to spread nationwide? Liz's mentorship had literally launched Jessica's career. To see that kind of influence go nationwide was mind–boggling.

Liz continued, "The mentors will have been selected for their expertise, experience, communication skills, and most importantly, for their ability to leave their egos at the door.

"There will be quarterly meetings with speakers and networking. In a perfect world, every mentee will get a booklet on how to work with mentors and how to get the most out of their experience. In addition, there will be educational material on the website and books available to those in the program."

Liz stopped, pondering the board.

"So why haven't you started this?" Jessica blurted. It seemed like it was a no–brainer. Who wouldn't want a mentor like Liz?

"Well, it's a matter of resources." She turned around to face the literacy wall. "All of this needs work too. There's only so much time in the day."

"But," Jessica thought frantically, "There's nothing LIKE the Invisible Brain Trust out there. There's not a formal mentorship for women available, at least not one I could find when you invited me to do this. No one is working on women's mentorship."

Liz frowned. "True, but there are women connecting with women more and more. BUT if someone can't read, they have absolutely no need for anything else. There is a fundamental need that isn't being met. Without reading you're only surviving."

Jessica looked between the two boards, frowning. "Mentorship and teaching. Education." She felt a tickle of an idea in the back of her head.

"You can't mentor every woman in America, so you're recruiting your friends and former co-workers."

"True, I'm casting a net."

"And if you could somehow convince all these women to mentor literacy, one-on-one tutoring would actually be something that would waste their time, squander their expertise."

Liz frowned, "I don't understand what you mean."

"If your high-powered CEO friends decided to spend their free time one-on-one tutoring English, it wouldn't be the most efficient use of their intelligence, experience, and specialty. Like if a computer programmer could design a program to teach everyone to read, but decides to spend his time helping one individual instead."

Liz thought for a moment and nodded. "I don't 100% agree, but I do think that I get what you're saying."

"Do these programs have to be mutually exclusive? What if part of the IBT program was for the next generation to learn mentoring skills by volunteering at their local library?"

Liz pivoted from the wall to face Jessica. "That's an interesting idea!"

Jessica blushed. "It just makes sense. You have mentors that are teaching leadership to at least one woman and maybe more than one. Part of leading is teaching. And teaching others how to read is something that can be done through any local library program... Completely scalable to a nationwide mentorship program."

Liz was hastily scribbling on the whiteboard making a large square with LITERACY CONNECTION printed in the middle and arrows shooting out from there with benefits and ideas to nestle one mission inside of the other... The board and the exact words were obscured by Liz's head, and Jessica let her eyes wander over the boards, coming to rest on the far wall. Those little boxes and lines. She stepped closer to it.

"Are you building a house?" she asked suddenly, but instantly saw she was wrong. There was a dotted line running through a larger box with the note *take down wall?* next to it.

Liz looked over in surprise. "Oh! No. We're moving."

Note From Robbie:

Over the course of my career, I have come to love the collaboration process. I cannot express how much I value and appreciate the input of others. Why? Because a symphony cannot be performed by one player. There must be a harmony of different ideas, skill sets, and talents to bring together one perfect piece of music – or business.

Collaboration contributes to success because it forces you to have a full 360-degree view of your project. It makes you take in other perspectives to see beneath the shiny surface. It keeps you from having a myopic view of one tiny aspect, one tree in the landscape, when collaboration requires you to see the whole forest.

There are, however, two things to be aware of when you seek collaboration. First, is that you must be open and willing to hear everyone's input. Don't take criticism personally. This isn't about you; this is about the success of your project, and you have to be open to new ideas and ugly truths. Only by hearing objections and complimentary ideas will your project have the best chance of success.

The second thing to bear in mind, is that there is only one decision maker. You seek out other ideas and opinions, but the whole project is not executed by committee. Innovation by committee is an oxymoron. It doesn't exist. At some point someone has to take charge to get things accomplished. If it is your project, it is your decision. Full stop.

Chapter 24
Embrace the Change

Liz looked from Jessica to the notes on the wall... "Oh! No. We're moving." She felt a smile touch her lips as she remembered the home that Brad had bought for them.

Their flight to LA had been a fast, secret thing, like two kids sneaking off for an adventure before dinner. They had left at the crack of dawn and come back before sunset, a whirlwind of activity bookended with airports and planes.

Brad had rented a car, driving slowly through his dream neighborhood, performing a gradual, deliberate real estate strip tease before finally coming to a stop in front of the most immaculate home on the block.

The yard was beautifully landscaped with water-saving plants arranged along the path to the door. The house itself was beige and blue, with board and batten exterior. The porch lights were on to welcome them.

Inside was a masterpiece. Each room had hardwood floors and wide, light filled windows. The high ceilings and open floor plan made the space feel enormous. The kitchen was outfitted with all the latest appliances and the largest island she had ever seen.

Liz, for her part, had tried desperately to quell the little voice inside. The one that noted every traffic delay and sign of urban decay. Touring the house had stilled the voice in a way that Liz's willpower had not. The little objecting voice was dumbfounded, staring in awe at the cathedral of light, stone, wood, and trees. This was theirs?

She had let Brad lead her from one room to the next. He held her hand, slowly revealing the dream they had made when their marriage was in its infancy, come to life. She had felt a growing excitement and elation as her eyes discovered each impeccable detail.

"Who owned this?" she wondered out loud. "And why would they sell?"

"As far as I understand, the owners were the kind of people who renovate houses, live in them, and sell them when they are ready for a new palette."

Liz had run her finger across the smooth granite kitchen counter. "That's insane."

Brad had met her eyes, a smile twitching on his lips. "You build successful businesses and then sell them. Some people would say *that's* insane."

Liz had tilted her head at him, smiling. "Did you just call me pot or kettle?"

They had kissed and hugged in the kitchen before heading out to the backyard, speckled in flowers and dancing shadows from the trees overhead. The flight back had been a verbal retouring of the home, reciting each detail to each other.

Jessica was staring at her wide-eyed and curious. Behind her were the dozens of notes and drawings she and Brad had drawn and discussed over the course of several days. The house had caught in her imagination like a fishhook. She came back to these drawings and the life they were going to live in it over and over again. Liz realized she had missed a question.

"Sorry, what?"

"Where is it?"

"Santa Monica."

Jessica looked puzzled for a moment and then the city clicked into place in her mental geography. "Oh! I didn't realize you were going to *move* move." There was an expression on her face that Liz couldn't immediately place.

She took Jessica's arm and spun her toward the wall. "I was really against the idea of moving to LA, but this house is *amazing*. Let me show you."

Liz pointed out the foyer and described the light and the vaulted ceilings. She verbally walked Jessica into the kitchen and living area that opened up to the beautiful patio just bringing the outside in... She enthusiastically described every detail, even the playroom for the grandkids.

"I guess you'd want to be closer to them," she gestured to the room marked playroom.

"Frankly, not this close. But, I won't be there fulltime, not in the beginning. We're going to sell this house and move some things into an apartment here. I'll base out of that on the weekdays to keep my office and connections here. Eventually I'll get tired of that I'm sure, but that might be around the time that I close shop anyway."

Jessica stood silently regarding the whiteboard. Her shoulders were stiff and Liz suddenly realized that Jessica had not really asked a single question.

"Jessica? Are you okay?"

"Fine," she replied, flatly.

Liz felt her eyebrows draw together. She mentally scanned back through the conversation, trying to spot where things had gone wrong. It was all euphoria and excitement on her part but Jessica was clearly upset... A moment later, the answer dawned on Liz. She had been so caught up in herself that she never stopped to think that she had become Jessica's lifeline of sorts.

"Hey," Liz said, pulling Jessica into a hug. "You know I'll still be there for you, right?"

Liz felt Jessica's head bob in a nod. She wondered if Jessica was crying, and indeed, when Liz pulled back, she did see tears in her eyes. Liz teared up a little too.

"I have mentored many young women over the course of my career," Liz said, pulling Jessica to an office chair and taking the other. "I am still in touch with almost all of them, where ever they are in the world."

Jessica took a deep, cleansing breath, "I'm sorry," she dabbed her eyes with a Kleenex. "I don't know what's come over me. I don't think I realized how much I've come to depend on you. I really enjoy talking with you. I feel heard."

Liz nodded. It seemed like Jessica's best friend was more of a talker than a listener. Someone like Jessica needed to feel heard too.

"I'll be around a lot because I'll have the apartment here. There's also Skype, Facetime, texting, plain old phone calls. I'll still be here to listen and bounce stuff off of."

When Jessica left that day, she was still a bit subdued, but putting a brave face on it. Liz reflected on the conversation and realized she needed to work with Jessica more on her coping skills and not taking things too personally. Change is a wheel that is always turning, and you needed to be flexible to turn with it. Liz had some ideas she thought might work and began making a list of how to incorporate them into her time with Jessica.

Note From Robbie:

Change happens, regardless of our opinion or our efforts to stop it. We personally change, we age, we have experiences, we learn. The world changes too. What was socially acceptable yesterday, isn't today... How you perceive change and cope with it will greatly impact your long-term success.

When faced with change, there are generally two responses. The first is to fight it. This looks like complaining, refusing, digging in heels, or posting rants to social media about how good life used to be (last year, or 20 years ago, or two generations before you were born). In general, these types of people are afraid and don't know how to cope. Fear keeps them rigid, unable to move with the times.

The other opportunity (another word for change) response is to embrace it. These are the people who see change as an opportunity or an adventure. They are agile and flexible, willing to see where this change is going to take them. This kind of response is typical of people who seek out new jobs, travel to new destinations, and (in general) have a higher quality of life than their rigid counterparts.

If you are not sure which type of response you

have, a good litmus test is to look at your social media postings. Do you post about the past or the future? Do you talk about how things are terrible now or how great things are? If you discover a rigid mindset, the first step to fixing it is awareness – congrats! You have achieved it. The second step is to start saying Yes. To anything. Invited to a night on the town? Yes. Is there a new job opening at work? Yes... Start saying Yes to life and see where it takes you!

Chapter 25

Owning the Room

Holy crap. That worked! Jessica stood awkwardly on stage as the sales team applauded enthusiastically. She knew there was a small shocked smile on her face, but for once she didn't care. *It was a success!*

Her stomach had eaten itself with nerves the entire flight to Phoenix. The walk from her hotel room to the conference center had been like walking to the gallows. And just as she was about to step on stage, all the dread, all the fear, was swept away. What had replaced it was a tranquility, a small voice that was confident that she was ready. That she could do this.

She had practiced everything that had transpired on stage. The slides, the talking points, the jokes, the pauses for laughter, she was rehearsed for every possible second until now. Jessica had never rehearsed for applause and found she was absolutely delighted to stand in it.

Now I see why Liz loves this!

She stepped off stage and into the shadows where Ken was waiting for her. "Great job!" he said and Jessica immediately recognized that this was the most genuine compliment he had ever given her.

"Thank you," she said, smiling broadly. She wondered how long she could hold onto this feeling.

On stage the MC was assuring the crowd that they would hear more about her product line in the technical discussion tomorrow. The Q&A session would officially end the gauntlet tomorrow, but for the first time Jessica wasn't worried about it. She was an expert on this product. They wouldn't be able to stump her. Best of all, they were welcoming and embracing her contribution.

It didn't appear that anyone would insist on their questions being answered now (someone had called up to the stage earlier in the day and forced an awkward situation) and the MC was busy introducing the next speaker. Jessica took the opportunity to slip out of the wings and discreetly head for the water station at the back of the room.

In the back, the water pitchers glistened with condensation that had gathered on the outside of the metal. Jessica hastily poured her water and drank down half the glass, giving herself a case of brain freeze. She wasn't sure she had drunk anything all day – convinced when it was her time to present she would have a painful need for the restroom. The cold water tasted better than anything now – brain freeze or not.

"Great presentation," a man murmured behind her. Jessica almost dropped her glass, whirling.

A tall man with dark hair was smiling behind her. In the shadows she wasn't sure about the color of his clothes, never mind his eyes, but he had a killer smile.

"Uh. Thanks," Jessica smiled, hesitantly. "Are you a salesman?"

"Not exactly," he whispered and dropped her a wink. "Can I buy you a drink later?"

Jessica felt her head involuntarily snap back in surprise. Simultaneously, her heart speed up faster than it had before she stepped on stage. It galloped so fast she thought that this mystery man might be able to hear it. He was grinning at her reaction in any case.

"What's your name?" she asked, stalling for time.

"Stephen."

Jessica bit her lip. What would Sarah do? Or Liz? Probably two very conflicting things. "Sure. Find me at the reception."

The rest of the afternoon went by in a blur. Jessica had glanced around discreetly when the lights were turned back up, but she hadn't spotted the mystery man. *It was dark!* she scolded herself. *You don't even know what color shirt he was wearing!*

It wasn't until that moment that it dawned on her that she had no idea what this guy even looked like. He was tall. He had dark hair. He had a great smile. Everything else had been shadows. She giggled to herself and then put it out of her mind. It was going to be his responsibility to find her after hours. For now, she had work to do.

And there was no shortage of work.

A parade of salespeople had come over to introduce themselves. Her mind boggled at the sheer idea of remembering all of the names, but on top of the names and the niceties, Jessica began to form a fairly strong opinion of these employees. They were confident, they understood how things worked, and they had ideas on how to make the company work better.

At first, she had struggled to take notes. After an hour she had wished for a voice recorder. And the people and the ideas just kept coming! There were pie-in-the-sky projects, ones that would never be financially feasible, but there were at least thirty, timely and viable products, suggestions, and tweaks. It was a brilliant storm of ideas and insights flash flooding over her.

When the woman in front of her paused for a breath, Jessica seized the opportunity to get to the bottom of her sudden popularity. "What you are suggesting is a really great systems hack. It sounds like you've been part of the company for years and have been to these sales meetings before – which means you are excellent at what you do. Out of curiosity, have you thought of talking to the technologies vice president? I think he's here if you want me to introduce you."

The woman waved a dismissive hand and chuckled, "Oh, I know Scott. At least, I know him as much as anyone does. He's definitely not interested in anyone's ideas but his own."

Jessica smiled, puzzled. "I feel like there's a story here that I missed. This is my first project with the company."

"Yeah, I bet that's not a story they tell around the headquarters water tank. Let's just say that someone asked too many questions and pushed back a little too hard and there was a scene. After that, communication just shut down between the salesforce and the tech department...

Jessica tried to place this new information in with what she had seen of Scott and how these "celebration events" worked. "I'm sorry to hear that."

She shrugged, "HQ has been distant. They wave from their private jets as they fly over us. Obviously they don't want to hear from us little folk. But *you*," she swung her shoulder forward to indicate Jessica, "are obviously listening *and* are getting things done. You, my dear, understand the products and the fact that you got anything done is a miracle. You are now my go-to person because you might hear it and do something about it."

Jessica didn't quite know what to say. "Thanks. I'll try to live up to that?"

Dinner flew by, in which Jessica endured some light ribbing from Ken. He had seen her popularity with the sales team. In typical Ken fashion, he had likened her to the best zookeeper in the zoo, feeding and petting all the egos in the menagerie. Jessica had shrugged it off, understanding exactly why the sales team preferred to speak to her and being proud to have earned their respect.

After dinner was the cocktail hour and she solemnly promised herself to drink nothing but coke with a lime garnish all night. There would be no repeat of that horrible scene at the prior conference. This was business, not her personal life.

The string of sales people continued, a blur of ideas and enthusiasm. She was doing a better job now of collecting names, quick bullet points and their home offices so she could follow back after the weekend was over. It was invigorating, and although Jessica knew implementing any of this would be an uphill battle, each person still deserved her attention and respect.

It seemed that Jessica blinked and the woman

in front of her magically morphed into the man from the water pitchers. Contrary to her fears, she recognized him right away. He was a little older than she had first thought, and was wearing a blue button down shirt the exact color of his eyes.

"Buy you that drink?"

Jessica held up her almost full glass of coke and smiled. "I'm doing great, thanks though."

"Ah, the next one then," he seemed embarrassed to have made the offer and Jessica wracked her brain to ease the conversation along.

"Did you do any golfing today?"

"Um. No. I couldn't get a tee-time."

Jessica frowned. Everyone who wanted to play had been paired and scheduled months ago. A piece suddenly clicked into place. "You're not actually with my company, are you?"

He leaned forward, eye dancing with amusement, "Shh! Do you want to get me kicked out?"

Jessica started laughing with disbelief. "Why on earth would you crash this?"

"Always good to know what is happening in the industry," he shrugged nonchalantly.

"Corporate espionage? Seriously?" she laughed again. "Aren't you blowing your cover right now?"

"Not espionage, nothing too secret actually goes on at these meetings. But recruiting? I'm always looking for new talent."

Jessica cocked an eyebrow at him. "See anything you like?" A shocked little part of her psyche couldn't believe she was having this conversation. The rest of her was delighted.

He nodded solemnly. "Very much so. I'm Steven by the way."

Jessica shifted her phone and drink to shake his hand. "Nice to meet you."

Her hand came away with a square business card in it... He caught her eye and nodded towards the small group of people waiting to speak to her. "Your fans await you. Call me some time."

Jessica smiled, not a bit embarrassed that she was blushing. "I will."

Note From Robbie:

In this chapter, Jessica is surrounded by new ideas. Some are completely crazy, some are reasonable, and some are nothing short of brilliant. People are sharing their ideas with her because she has proven that she 1.) listens and 2.) takes action. They don't know the history of how she got to where she is, all they see is the results.

Additionally, Jessica is reaping the benefit of being an expert on this topic – in the form of recognition by an outside talent scout. There was a time, early in this story when Jessica would have shied away from that encounter. She would have closed the door with a resounding No. She was so busy trying to survive in her job she couldn't see the opportunities around her. What she has learned is that you don't have to say "Yes" immediately, you can tuck away these connections with a Maybe Later.

Knowing when to hold 'em and when to fold 'em is a skill that is learned over time and with practice. Often in business you need to play your cards close. You need to hold onto trade secrets or make a play for a new position. Sometimes you need to tuck a card away until the day you need it.

Chapter 26

Bring in the Experts

"You can always tell a 'Liz Meeting' by the toys!" Tillie cackled in her booming voice... She was tall, reasonably fit (for pushing 60) and grey haired, unlike many of the other women in the meeting.

The rest of the room chuckled in appreciation. Even Marie's slightly digitized voice was laughing through the Skype interface.

"Am I late?" she asked scooping up a koosh ball from the table and pulling it back, shooting it in Liz's direction, rubber band style.

Liz caught the flying projectile deftly, "Nope, waiting on two more." Jessica was supposed to be here. She was the test case, and it would make it harder if she didn't show.

Tillie took a seat next to Nancy, who would be putting her extensive law knowledge at their disposal today. Nancy knew her stuff and wasn't shy to speak her mind, but she also had that element that Liz was looking for in potential mentors, the ability to put her own ego aside. Nancy would never grandstand, never put someone down to hear her own thunder.

Next to Nancy was a space that had been left empty for Marie, who was peering through a computer screen mounted on the wall. The space and angle let Marie see down into the conference table and the wall beyond, where the notes would go later.

Marni sat on the other side of the gap. She was the rare sort of CPA, the kind that could break complex concepts down to laymen's terms. She actually saw people, not just the numbers that accompanied them. Her practice had always been ridiculously successful, and Liz suspected she would also be a good mentor for the very same reason.

The last two spaces were for Ann and… *there she is!*

Jessica came into the room with her shoulders back and a wide grin on her face. She introduced herself around the table, even giving Marie's screen a wave, and gave Liz a hug in the rounds. Jessica was owning it. Liz couldn't see a hint of the girl who had confessed she wasn't at the table. This Jessica was confident and Liz couldn't have been happier.

Ann slipped in a moment later, and Liz caught everyone's attention with a little trick she had been using for years. She gathered up three koosh balls and began to juggle, making them start slowly and speeding up as she got the feel. Soon every eye was on her and the whirling balls until one slipped, sailing past her fingers and plopping against the far wall. There was a chorus of applause and laughter and Liz launched into her presentation.

She hadn't prepared anything too fancy for the meeting. A few handouts with bullet points but not a full-on PowerPoint, dim the lights and stay silent for the show kind of thing. Liz had been tempted, her secret obsession was PowerPoint, but she knew these ladies would be bored with it. On top of which, she wanted their ideas, not their agreement. In Liz's experience, big presentations didn't really foster conversation, as if the act of creating the presentation finalized it, making it no longer up for discussion.

Liz read the body language of the group as she described her vision of women mentoring women. Ann leaned forward and Nancy was taking notes. Jessica watched her, smiling and nodding. When she got to the part about literacy, Liz noted some frowns, some confusion. *Hmmm. This should be interesting.*

She wrapped up her presentation by drawing horizontal and vertical lines on the board on the far wall. In each of the resulting squares she wrote a topic:

Purpose	Structure
Finances	Action Items

"Okay so now you know what I have been playing around with and I really want us to explore the good, the bad, and the ugly...You know I love you and I value your opinions, so fire away. I need your thoughts!"

Tillie was first to speak up, she was a consultant who was paid for her opinion and ability to express it, after all. "I've mentored my fair share of both young women and men over the years. Some of them were amazing and others just did not "click" for a variety of reasons," she shrugged. "So what's the end goal? What do you see this whole thing accomplishing in the end?"

Liz didn't hesitate. "Ultimately? I want fair wages, a fair representation of women in management positions, and a generation of strong women succeeding on their own terms. While I'm at it, free birth control, universal access to safe, affordable abortions, and a goddamn woman president."

"Okay, I think we're on the same page then," Tillie smiled... "Put Goddamn Woman President under Purpose, why don't ya?"

"I think that's a little too political," Nancy said. "You've got a basic 501(c)3 structure for mentoring and literacy. If you get too far into politics, you've got a whole other filing you'll need to go under."

"I agree," Marni piped up. "The tax benefits in a 501(c)3 are amazing, but that can get yanked in a heartbeat if we are messing around in politics. Any money gained would need to go the mentoring and literacy programs. Speaking of, how do you plan on financing this?"

"Let's classify a G.D. Woman President as our super-secret mission," Liz laughed. "Let's not get too carried away. As for the finances, there will be a nominal fee for the young women seeking mentorship – just so they have skin in the game. From there, we'll need to pitch sponsors."

Ann looked up from furious note taking. "That should be a snap. Look at the demographics of these two groups! They both have what retailers are looking for, head of household women with disposable income." Ann had recently retired from a career in marketing. She could SEO the hell out anything.

"What are the costs going to be, anyway?" This was Jessica, who looked like she regretted speaking up the moment all those eyes turned towards her... To her credit, she took a breath and soldiered on. "Mostly marketing and event planning, right?"

Tillie frowned, scanning her bullet points. "You mean mentors aren't paid?"

Liz laughed, "Seriously, Tillie, you want to be paid? The kinds of women we want mentoring are at the end of very successful careers. What amount of money would tempt someone to mentor? Versus what we could raise? It would be laughable. No, a mentor needs to mentor because she wants to, not because we can entice her with a $100 stipend. It's paying it forward that we all need to do and set the example for the next generation to do the same."

"Yeah," Ann agreed. "I'd be embarrassed to take money for it anyway."

"There may be legal ramifications to that as well. If you are paid to give mentorship advice and give bad direction." Nancy made a note on her list. "I'll check it out."

"I think we need to rebrand this though," Ann sounded apologetic. "Invisible Brain Trust is catchy, but it takes explaining and it's not going to attract the younger demographic at all."

Liz frowned. She hadn't thought about that. "I'd be sad to let it go, but I see your point. Any ideas what it should be?"

The ideas piled onto the board. They were bouncing around between the different quadrants of the board, but Liz didn't mind that. These women were all experts in their field and those talents covered each section.

"How are we going to pair mentors with mentees?" Marie asked from the computer screen.

She continued to muse, "Mentees? Is that even a word?"

"We could probably tweak that," Ann made another note to herself. "Mentorees? Is that better?"

"But is there criteria to match these pairs?" Marie asked again.

"For now I thought we'd keep it organic. Arrange meetings and have a mixer for people to talk and connect. I expect in the beginning we may have an imbalance of more young women than mentors. Some mentors may decide to take on a flock; that'll be their choice."

"Okay, this is my last push back, and then I'll keep my peace," Tillie prefaced. "Are we sure there are women who want this? Are you building something that no one is going to show up to? Is this your field of dreams, Liz? If you build it will they come?"

"Oh, I can speak to that!" Jessica answered enthusiastically. "When I met Liz I was nothing but a glorified note-taker for my department meetings. What's it been Liz, a year? Fourteen months?"

Liz nodded, "Something like that."

"I have led a new product line for my company that launches next month. I'm suddenly being flown to company conferences to give speeches, the sales team loves me, and," she paused to address Liz directly, "I forgot to tell you this part, I was even approached by a head hunter for a competing company!"

Liz grinned. It didn't surprise her one bit that others would start to take notice.

"Bottom line," Jessica continued, "mentorship has been life-changing for me. If I had known where to find one earlier, I would have shown up every day, hat in hand, asking for one."

There were no more questions about purpose after that. It was quickly agreed that literacy would also be an integral part of the program. After all, what teaches you to put aside your ego and dial up your patience better than teaching someone to read? The literacy program would be mandatory for the women receiving mentorship, so they could continue the giveback loop, but would also be highly recommended for new mentors to get back to "beginner's mind."

Note From Robbie:

Hand in hand with collaboration, is the solid benefit of networking... You meet lots of people who are experts in various fields and you develop a relationship with them and, wow, the collaborative possibilities are amazing. Most small businesses fail for lack of FOCUS, plus lack of planning, lack of foresight, and understanding of the marketplace. The legal and financial pieces alone can sink a business if it isn't handled carefully in the very beginning.

It is important to build a team of experts you can consult with. These are people you need to trust, because they have a deep understanding of their specialty. You cannot be an expert in everything, you need other people to contribute to your overall success.

Leverage your network and peers to find people who are excellent at what they do and you can return that favor at some point. I really believe what goes around, comes around.

Chapter 27

Set the Expectations

Jessica's heart thundered in her chest as she scanned the email from IT a second time. Words like "delayed" and "errors" popped out like frightening jack-in-the-boxes screaming *BOO!* at her. The launch of her product line was less than 10 days away, and suddenly it looked a million years off... *How did this happen? What had she missed?*

She hadn't had the slightest indication that there was a problem. She had delivered everything on their timeframe. How could they drop the ball like this? And to make things worse, it looked like they were pointing the finger of blame at her! This just did not make any sense.

The marketing department had press releases circulating and the printed materials had already shipped. The sales people were already taking pre-orders. How could the technical department not deliver? How could they expect her to put the brakes on now? It would be like trying to stop the Titanic and her project would sink with her career on board.

Jessica glanced nervously over at Ken's office. He and Charlene had been in meetings multiple times in the last few days. They seemed to be going steadily downhill. She had no idea what they were working on, but Charlene had looked like a deer in the headlights in recent days. Ken had been down right stormy towards everyone.

"Alan? You there?"

"Yeah."

"Do you know what's going on in Ken's office? With Charlene?"

Alan's head popped over the wall. "No one has said for sure, but the grapevine is that she lost a major supplier last week. I think they've been scrambling to win them back or find a new one."

"That's bad," Jessica said, wondering how bad things would get for her if the product line didn't launch next week. Or worse, if Ken believed IT that the delay was her fault.

"Really bad," Alan agreed. "I think –"

But whatever Alan thought was cut off by rising voices in Ken's office. The door was slightly ajar and things were getting downright nasty. Through the window she could see that Charlene was giving it right back to Ken...

Jessica was on her feet, staring openly at the confrontation going down just 20 feet away. A glance to her left revealed Alan was still standing too, transfixed by the spectacle in their boss's office. She felt like her muscles were twisted taunt, her stomach churning acid. She hated fighting. Hated it. Without realizing it, her eyes began darting for an escape path, an excuse, any reason to be anywhere else on the planet.

The voices continued to rise, culminating in Ken yelling, "DON'T LET THE DOOR HIT YOU ON THE WAY OUT!"

Charlene was out the door shouting a trail of expletives behind her. She saw Jessica and Alan standing agog and she paused for a second before flipping them the bird and continuing to her cubicle. Charlene scooped up her purse, tossed her company ID on her desk and was gone.

In the wake of the fight, Jessica suddenly felt very exposed... Ken stood in the doorway of his office watching Charlene go. His gaze lingered in the direction of the Cube Farm. Jessica glanced at Alan and they both hastily dove into the cover of their cubicles. On the computer screen loomed the damning email from IT. Jessica bit her lip and sent a hasty "911" text to Liz.

"Wow, yeah that would be unnerving," Liz

sympathized. Jessica was parked down the street from the office, holding onto her phone as if it was a lifeline.

"Do you think I can force IT to get the project done on time without getting Ken involved? Like go bribe them with pizza every day for lunch and dinner or something? Or!" Jessica spitballed, "maybe I could talk marketing into delaying their side. I don't know. I feel like I'm on a speeding train and IT has just dynamited the bridge. I'm going to fail. I'm going to get fired. *Oh my God!* I don't want to lose my car!"

"Woah there. You have super powers, Anxiety Girl. Make sure you use them for good, not evil."

Jessica smiled wanly. This was not the first time she'd been accused of that.

"Let me tell you a story. It's a moment I'm not proud of, but... it's appropriate for this situation, okay?"

"Okay," Jessica agreed curiously.

"I was working for a consulting firm, and we were automating the collection of parking tickets for a couple major cities on the east coast. We were a software company and we were implementing all of this new technology. It was my project and as we started there was a lot of resistance to it. It took a long time to get all the major players on board.

"We were getting closer and closer to the finish line and there was going to be this huge launch and press conference, 'finally the city was going to be able to do all this stuff with tickets, blah blah blah,' and we had our press person ready to go.

"A couple of nights before the launch it became very apparent that the shining solution we had sold the city, technology–wise, was not going to be ready on time.

"I couldn't demand that it be done. What we tried to do was cut back the scope of what was being delivered... I was killing these poor people in the IT department doing all the work. And, at the same time I was telling the city, 'oh, everything is just dandy,' not letting them know that we were on a wing and a prayer.

"Anyway, I don't know why I let the situation go as far as I did. I guess I had faith in this technology team of mine, that they would find a way to make it look like it was working, even if it wasn't. A little smoke and mirrors. The night before the big press conference, it was clear that it wasn't going to happen.

"I got so pissed off at myself, I kicked a trash can and broke my toe. I was like, 'What am I going to do? How can I stop this?' The train had already left the station. All these people were going to be there. How did I let it get to this point?'

"And I still didn't pull the plug! I didn't know how! The next morning, we were all at the court early. I took my senior implementation guy down to the basement of the court house– now this was pre-9/11, pre-terrorism, and said, 'We've got to do something. Let's kill the power.'"

"You are kidding me!" Jessica gasped.

"No! We find the breaker, whatever you call it, and he's trying to talk me out of it. I'm like, okay, here's what you're going to do. I'm going to go upstairs and we're going to synchronize our watches. And in however many minutes, you're going to pull that switch. And we're going to go, 'Oh my God, we have no power. Darn! Press conference cancelled.'

"So we planned a felony rather than cancel the press conference and postpone the launch of the product."

"What happened?" Jessica asked.

"Well, I got lucky. About 15 minutes before the 'power outage' was supposed to happen, the IT team found a smoke and mirrors fix. It all came together. Otherwise I might have spent the better part of 1998 in jail."

Jessica tried to imagine Liz in jail. Or, so panicked that she would cut power to entire courthouse rather than admit her product was late. She held that image up next to the woman who had masterfully hosted a brainstorming meeting of her peers to dissect her latest brainchild. Jessica could almost see the evolution of a career, of a strong woman in the space between. It left her feeling hopeful for her own prospects.

"I guess my point," Liz continued over the

phone, "is when you don't manage expectations appropriately, and aren't willing to be transparent with the problems, eventually extreme measures look like completely rational decisions.

"You also need to stay very close to the technology folks so that if problems arise you can offer places that can be cut without killing the whole project. I think you need to go see them and sit down to understand where the problems are and what solutions you can help implement. You and the Technology team need to be hand in hand on this product. Neither of you wants there to be unsolvable problems.

"I need to be transparent with Ken."

"You and the IT head need to meet with Ken together once you have come up with a solution and let him know what you both think the impact will be."

Jessica nodded and thanked Liz before turning her car back in the direction of the office. The image of a flawed, panicked Liz was probably the most inspirational gift Liz had ever given her. It meant that Liz hadn't always had all the answers, hadn't known all the lessons. Jessica was suddenly calm, sure that if she wasn't leadership material now, she could be in the future.

Note From Robbie:

Over my career in the software business it was

always a challenge to set expectations and buy-in on every level. In a company with many projects and many priorities, getting everyone to agree – and remember they agreed – to a timeline is difficult.

When you successfully manage to set expectations, several things happen. First, and most obviously, everyone knows what to expect. This might be a "duh" to you, but for some people juggling a million different priorities and projects, agreeing to expectations automatically gives a project higher visibility on the "to-do" list. It is best to have the expectations in writing, so if there are unforeseen staff changes or other hiccups, there is a documented plan to refer to.

The second thing that happens with set expectations is that it levels the playing field. There is one vision, one mission, one goal. There isn't pulling rank, there isn't trying to weasel someone into doing your work for you. It's a level playing field because everyone knows what they are expected to contribute to get the project completed. Like a soccer team, the players each have their positions and their expected duties when the ball comes their way.

The third thing that happens with set, written expectations is that you have to get buy-in from all the major stakeholders. They have a chance to put in their opinion, explain their particular challenges and state what they need to get the job done. Through this process they grant buy-in to seeing the project to completion.

Chapter 28
Dare to Disagree

Jessica was appalled. Of the team of four that was supposed to be assigned to her project, only one was actually doing the work. The other three had been reassigned.

"Your email didn't say that it was just you now."

"I thought you knew."

Charles, a serious geek, was the epitome of every computer science major she had met in college. He was superior and confident, as long as he was in his cubicle, discussing computer programing. He wasn't big on eye contact, or social skills in general, but he was an expert at what he did.

"Can you get them back on this project?"

"No."

"Why not?" Talking to him was like pulling teeth.

"Because I don't assign priority," Charles said exasperated.

"What's more important than this?" Jessica asked, incredulous.

"What isn't?"

Jessica wanted to take him by the shoulders and shake him. Hard. "The launch is next week." Charles was unmoved. He clicked his mouse on a new email, not bothering to look at her. "Who is assigning priority?"

"VP of Technology."

"If I get the rest of the team back, can you still make the deadline?"

"Maybe."

"Thanks, Charles." Jessica fought to keep the sarcasm from her voice as she turned and stalked out of IT...

She went straight to Ken's office. There was no way that the VP of Technology would reprioritize her project without support from Ken. The door was open and he was angrily, typing something on his computer, jabbing each key on the keyboard with extra emphasis. Jessica tapped on the door frame.

Ken looked up, surprised to see her. "Give me just a moment."

Jessica stood awkwardly in the doorway until Ken clicked his mouse a few times and then gestured for her to enter. She closed the door behind her.

"I need your help," she said without preamble. "There's been some sort of miscommunication in the IT department. Instead of four people working to code the product line into the sales software, there's only one. I'm being told the project was deprioritized by the VP of Technology." Jessica thought for a moment about Charles and his demeanor before adding, "I don't know if that's true."

"Do we need four people?"

"They're estimating a month delay with just one person working on it."

"That's unacceptable."

"That's why I'm here. I figured you wouldn't want me barging into the VP of Technology's office without consulting you for a better way."

Ken gave her the ghost of a smile.

"No. I'll handle this. Someone probably pulled rank on a project not due for months. I'll talk to him."

Later that afternoon Jessica received an email from Ken. "IT underestimated resources required.

You're back on track." Jessica breathed a sigh of relief.

Note From Robbie:

Women often find it very difficult to disagree with a colleague much less managers up the food chain. We are taught that it is not polite to disagree, so rather than be direct and potentially cause a conflict, women seem to find obscure and circuitous routes to disagreeing without actually doing it. We complain to people who are not in positions to solve the issue. We send anonymous notes. We voice disagreement as someone else's opinion that we are just in the unfortunate position of having to share.

In this case, Jessica needed to advocate for her project and her options were to A.) Cheerfully beat the indifferent Charles to death with her shoe, B.) March into the VP of Technology's office and demand the team be reassigned back to her project, or C.) Go to her direct manager and ask for him to have a peer-to-peer discussion with the VP of Technology. Note that in this case, the best option was the one with the least potential for emotional outbursts.

There is such a thing as constructive conflict. A healthy disagreement can delve into department challenges and illuminate issues you were not aware of. The hallmark of constructive conflict is that the team has a level of mutual trust and respect. If you beat a co-worker with a shoe (whether he deserves it or not) or show up unannounced and make demands, this erodes the trust and respect of the team. Once the trust and respect is lost, it is hard to recover.

You can use the system to manage your responsibilities. You can delegate up as well as down. Delegating this responsibility to Ken wasn't a failure, it was the most direct and efficient path to conflict resolution. The wisdom is in determining when you are seeking help vs. giving up on your own ability to solve the problem.

Chapter 29

Celebrate

"I can't believe you're leaving!"

It was probably the 50th time that Liz had heard that sentiment in the last day and a half, and at least the second time she had heard it from Tillie. Tillie had said it as she was coming in, and now, as she left a bit tipsy and clutching her newly claimed goodies, she gave Liz another bear hug. "I'm going to miss you!"

"I'll still be around," Liz assured her.

Tillie gave her one last squeeze and then wandered out to find her husband and their safe ride home. Liz smiled after her. Brad had been right. This party was a good idea.

Liz and Brad had hosted regular parties up until

about two years ago. Somewhere along the line the entertaining had moved from fun to chore. The expectation and demands were too much, and they had made the decision together to pass the baton. But when the party schedule had gone dark, they found that there was an unforeseen consequence. Long standing invitees thought they were snubbed, that the party was continuing without their presence. An email to the regulars (a much longer list than Liz had realized) set the record straight.

And here they were again; all things come around. The party had been Brad's idea, a way to get say goodbye and at the same time reconnect to their extensive list of friends, acquaintances, and business connections. In the tradition of all their parties, they had asked their friends to bring items for donation. It worked like a charm, home décor items appeared for donation to Habitat for Humanity, clothes came tagged for Dressed for Success. This time Liz also included a call for easy reader books, and a good number of almost new and lovingly thumbed children's books had appeared.

Of course, these books were meant for children. But through her involvement with the literacy center, Liz had come to discover that a fair number of adults were motivated to learn so they could read to their children. These books would be read to countless children, Liz had no doubt.

Liz looked at the pile of donations that had come in with the guests over the last day and a half. Tomorrow two teenage boys would sort through it and get it to the appropriate donation centers. Additionally, the team from Sort and Pack was coming to tackle the house. After 30 years of living in their home, it would take nothing short of professional help to pry their history from the house.

But first... Liz smiled bitter-sweetly at her topsy-turvy home. The caterer had laid out an impressive table of warming dishes filled with small bites. The kitchen had been converted to a make shift champagne bar. But even with these odd additions, other missing pieces showed.

A blank space in a line of small framed pictures, where she had given the favored piece to an old friend. A table lamp no longer on a side table. The pile of extraneous entertaining dishes that had slowly shrunk until three unmatched plates had remained. The remembrances of good friendships, conversations, a lifetime of souvenirs had been given to the friends who would appreciate them most.

Tucked away in their bedroom were the dog-eared pieces for Marie and Evan, and the special things that belonged to their marriage, but the rest had been up for grabs. Liz and Brad agreed, they would much rather see these physical manifestations of their memories in the hands of friends than strangers.

Whatever trinkets could find a good home, should. There was no guarantee that these things would belong in their new home, their new life.

In the backyard, someone had liberated a bottle

of champagne and was calling for a toast... People were calling for her to come and join them and Liz went, willingly enough. Outside, Brad held the spotlight, a glass outstretched toward her.

"My beautiful wife," Brad began. Liz noted his glassy eyes and hoped this wouldn't be too embarrassing. Nancy handed Liz a frothing glass of the bubbly and she took a nervous sip to fortify herself.

"You..." he paused, dragging it out, perhaps trying to decide what to say. Liz fought the urge to squirm. "...are my better half." Brad tipped his glass back abruptly and took a sip. He grinned and winked at her. The gathered group laughed in appreciation, the long-standing joke coming to a new conclusion. Brad always roasted Liz in a long winded speech, but tonight he had turned the tables, being ultra-brief. Liz returned his grin and wink.

When the gathering broke back into little groups of chatter, Nancy clinked her glass against Liz's. "To your future!"

"And to yours," Liz replied before taking a sip.

"So, with you moving to LA, what is going to happen with your business? And the mentorship program?"

"In the short-term not much is going to change. I'm keeping an apartment here in town to base out of. I'll be back up quite a bit as it's only an hour flight. I have speeches committed for the next six months at least. I'll slowly transition to LA, networking, and making connections there.

"As for the mentorship program, the goal is to be anywhere and everywhere. Cloud-based and nationwide, simultaneously. I think it will thrive where ever there are women willing to teach and wanting to learn."

Nancy nodded thoughtfully, "I can't get that meeting we had out of my head. I find myself reminiscing about the mistakes I made and what a young person in my industry needs to know." She smiled ruefully. "You can leave school with all the book knowledge in the world, but you need to know how to talk to people to succeed."

"I think you'll be a great mentor," Liz said reassuringly. "We are definitely moving forward with the project. Jessica was here earlier tonight. Did you see her?"

"I did!" Nancy said happily. "She told me that her product line launched on time and on budget. She was practically floating."

"Jessica is the classic Dorothy from the Wizard of Oz. She had the power the whole time; she just had to learn it for herself."

Nancy looked thoughtfully over the backyard. "I wish that women inherently knew their own power. It seems like we know it when we are young and some where along the line we are shamed out of it. Did you know I was a secretary for three years before I decided to go back to school and follow my passion?"

"I didn't know that!"

"I couldn't stand typing up other people's nonsense. It made my soul shrink. One day I just had enough. I enrolled in an accounting program. I was the only woman in my class."

Liz nodded, she knew about being the only woman in the room.

"When is your last night in town? I know you're going to be back and all of that, but when is the big move going to be?"

"Next Friday."

"Come over for dinner. Frank and I would love to have you. We can open a couple bottles of wine and say our farewells."

Liz nodded, touched. "We would love that."

Nancy made her way out, towing Frank, about an hour later. As the rest of the group said their goodbyes and trickled towards the door, Liz surveyed her home. It was a disheveled collection of happy memories. It also, for the first time, seemed like a space she was ready to move on from. Her new house, her new life, was waiting 300 miles south of here – and it was calling her home.

Note From Robbie:

Throughout my career I have seen a variety of ways to give closure to life's big and little milestones. From company launches to companies being shuttered. From weddings and baby showers to divorces and retirements. A celebration, to me, seems like the best way to gain closure.

When we plan a party, or have some sort of chocolate-based ritual, a celebration signals that one thing has ended so a new one can begin. It signals your sub-conscious that whatever event it was; it is now over. You gather your friends and say goodbye to one part of your life so that the next part can begin. It's cathartic.

I particularly find that a celebration puts a final exclamation point on a success. A party means you are done, that you passed the finish line, that you don't need to worry about it anymore. A celebration is important because it gives you the freedom to move forward to the next adventure!

Chapter 30

Gratitude

The wedding has taken over my apartment. Jessica thought as she shifted the newest box from the porch into the crowded living room. The big day was still two months out, and the living room looked like a combination storage/craft room for a lady inventing new uses for tulle and burlap.

Interspersed with successful centerpieces and not-so successful place cards were boxes of unwrapped presents. They had begun arriving ever since the save the date cards went out... Jessica checked the tag on the newly arrived package, hoping for a shipment of wine or a keg from BevMo to "accidentally" open. No such luck; Crate and Barrel.

Jessica had a solid bet that the mandolin slicer

on the gift registry would spend two years in a cupboard before going straight into a garage sale. Do not pass go. Do not waste your two hundred dollars. The wedding, the shower, the gift registry, and all the rest of the "celebration" were sheer madness.

"Sarah! You home?" she called out into the apartment, dropping her purse on a stack of pre-cut burlap piled on the couch and shedding little brown specks everywhere.

Her cat came out of her room and meowed at her, complaining in his cat way. "Heya Fluff Master. Whatchya complainin' about? Need some food?" He meowed back a little more insistently.

"Okay, okay."

When she flipped on the light in the room, she could see why the cat was peeved. She was suddenly peeved too. There were empty boxes piled on her bed. On closer inspection, there was a note from Sarah.

Ryan and I are going to Tahoe for the weekend. Had to get away from the wedding planning! Hope you have a great weekend!

Sarah

PS. People keep shipping us presents! I was about to toss these boxes but I realized they would be good for packing for your big move!

Jessica swore. Fluff Master gave her a disapproving

meow before wandering off to check out the food bowl.

"Oh, ha! Ha!" Jessica mimicked in a falsetto to an invisible audience. "People send me so many gifts I have to run away!" She tossed the note on the floor of her room and pushed the empty boxes into the space between the bed and the wall. With a workspace cleared, she opened her laptop and began hunting for a new place to live.

It wasn't that she was being pushed out that irked Jessica so much. She had agreed to move months ago. No, what irked her was that she had cheap rent in a decent neighborhood and in the three years since she and Sarah had signed the lease, the rent prices were going nowhere but up. She had been scanning the ads once a week and it really looked like she would have to choose between *cheap* and *decent.*

From her research she knew that she should be bringing in three times what she was paying out in rent. Anything more and it would look iffy to potential landlords and could possibly throw her finances out of tilt if there was some sort of disaster.

Technically, she made enough that she didn't need a roommate. But her finances were just at that tipping point of studio in a nice area or one-bedroom in an "eclectic" area. Jessica looked at the numbers again... *what if I asked for a raise?*

It was like a lightning bolt had struck nearby. The tiny hairs on her arms stood up.

She dove for her phone and sent a text off to Liz, "Any tips on asking for a raise?"

The answer was almost instantaneous. "Tons! And you DESERVE one! First research what people with your job title/duties make on the Internet. See what is average in this area."

A few keyword phrases later and Google coughed up a website that monitored pay rates for product managers. Jessica input her resume and hit "calculate."

Survey says...

"Oh!" Jessica felt like someone had punched her. Hard.

She scanned the page again and again. There was the graph. There was the average. And near the bottom, near the lowest paid, was the arrow indicating her income. In comparison to the rest of the product managers in the country, she was being grossly, disgustingly underpaid.

"Shit."

It had been tempting to quit. It had been tempting to get drunk. In the end, Jessica went for a run. And in her mind she let her inner monologue RAGE. She came up with angry scenarios involving her physically beating the hell out of Ken. She invented witty scenes where she eviscerated him verbally in front of the team.

When the anger ran out, the shame threatened to bowl her over, and she ran faster. How many people knew? And, no wonder no one took her seriously! She was so embarrassed she didn't know how she could walk into the office again, or worse, tell Liz.

So she ran some more. Jessica had left the house in running clothes, carrying a water bottle and a key to her apartment, with only a vague direction she planned to run in. That's it. Her phone and her computer were going to get some alone time. Plans and distances run/walk patterns were going to get a rest too.

She stopped by a playground near city hall and filled her water bottle when it ran dry. Her emotions, she realized, were running dry too. It no longer entertained her to imagine Ken's public humiliation at her hands. It no longer stung to think about her own plight. There was an acceptance coming, one that she hated but knew was true. She had failed to negotiate the job offer. Yeah, they lowballed her, but it was also her fault.

Jessica wandered around for a bit, catching her breath, stretching her legs. She was four miles from home, more or less. The city hall and police station parking lots were almost empty. Everyone had gone home for the weekend. The library still looked open though.

Jessica headed over, realizing that she was sweaty and her face was probably beet red, but deciding she didn't really care. She had an idea to do something good. Something she had intended to do for a while but hadn't really gotten around to it yet. Something that would turn this energy around and make it a positive memory.

Inside, the library was cool and quiet. There were plenty of adults and teenagers wandering the stacks, on their respective literary missions. Jessica made her way to the resources desk and waited patiently to be acknowledged by the librarian.

"How can I help you?"

"I'd like to volunteer for the literacy program."

The librarian smiled...

Note From Robbie:

Gratitude and giving is a very individual thing... Everyone has different reactions to life's events. Even as children we feel the joy of giving our parents or friend a gift that they genuinely seem to love and we feel all warm inside. That feeling is what we all crave and often forget it comes from GIVING and giving back.

There is another incredible side–effect of giving back: a feeling of empowerment. As a friend told me, "There was a time in my life that I was frustrated at work. It felt like nothing was getting done and the rest of the office was content with the status quo. I was miserable. So I took action and joined

Habitat for Humanity. Every weekend I would go out and work with 30-50 people to frame a house, or put a roof on, or sheathe walls. It lifted my spirit to see something getting done in the world and that my actions could have a tangible result at the end of the day."

If you are not volunteering yet, it's time to give it a try. Any kind of giving back can give you relief from stress, anger, fear, and frustration... It is giving, but the act of giving is for you, for your mental well-being.

Chapter 31

Channel Up

In all of the packing and hubbub, Liz realized she couldn't look at one more cardboard box. She picked up the phone and dialed Jessica, hoping for a distraction or a possible problem to solve. Now things had worked out splendidly. Jessica had been on her way to a day spa and had quickly made additional appointments to accommodate Liz. Brad had volunteered to take responsibility of overseeing the movers and she was happily sipping champagne in a spa waiting for her masseuse.

Jessica, Liz noted, looked comfortable in her surroundings. She was wrapped in a plush robe, her cheeks still flush from the hot tub. She had seemed preoccupied, but Jessica almost always had something on her mind. Liz was no one to judge on that account, she kept clicking on her phone to jot down a reminder every other minute. So much to do at home and with the mentoring and literacy projects, never mind speaking commitments. She was so excited about all of it.

"It was sort of anti-climactic, you know what I mean?" Jessica was saying. "I put a year of my life into developing and putting together this product line and now... it's just out there." She waved a hand vaguely. "It's done, but I won't know if it's a success for some time to come."

"Sounds like you didn't get any closure."

"Yeah! That's exactly right. I didn't even get like a note of thanks or a pat on the back or anything. It was just a click of a button."

"Has your boss talked to you about your next project yet?"

"Not really. They want me to monitor the product line for the next few months. I don't think they know what to do with me now." Jessica fidgeted a little, giving her fingers a close inspection. Liz had seen this before. Jessica was working her way up to something important. Liz wondered what she could say to make it easier for Jessica.

"Are you worried you won't have as high profile of a project next time?"

Jessica shook her head. "No, I have a feeling they are going to try and squeeze every ounce of brain power out of me."

"Hmmm." Liz tried to guess what was bothering Jessica. She too knew the sudden let down after a big project came to a close. It was one of the reasons she loved to throw a party, to put a final exclamation point on the success so she was free to move forward to the next adventure.

"Is that how you feel? Squeezed?"

Jessica smiled ruefully, "I guess that's a good word for it. Squeezed." She sat up straighter, turning more towards Liz. "Okay. I'm going to level with you. I made a mistake and I don't want a lecture, but I need help fixing it."

Liz bit back what she wanted to say, that she *never* lectured... Instead she said, "Lay it on me."

"I didn't negotiate my salary," Jessica grimaced, showing her clenched teeth. "I took the first offer. I know, I know, I'm an idiot. I didn't realize until I did the research to ask for a raise." Jessica dropped her eyes, focusing instead on the fluff of her robe. "So I made an appointment with my boss to discuss a raise and he refused the appointment because they 'only discuss raises in the first month of the year.'"

Jessica sounded completely dejected and Liz felt for her. "You're not alone, Jessica. Lots of women don't understand that they need to negotiate for the job – it's a big factor for why women make less than men. I think I've hardly hired a woman who hasn't apologized somehow in asking for her salary. We make excuses by saying 'I'm sure you can't afford it, but I really need...' versus a man who says, 'Look, I need $75K. I'm really worth $150K, but I'll do this job for $75K.'"

Jessica blinked at her. "You lowball women when you hire them?"

"No. I have a budget and a range I spend for a position. Sometimes it's just not the right fit and that's OK... It does not work out. However, women need to learn to stand up for themselves. I can't make an exception and coach a prospective female employee to ask for more money; that would be unfair and discrimination. I usually ask HR to tell a candidate that the position has a pay range of X and Y, so we don't waste each other's time. On the other hand, if you know the salary range going in is not enough for you, then you need to be honest that you want the job for certain experience or you just need a job, but you cannot expect someone to pay you more than the range without a good reason or because they like treating women well. It's a two-way street.

"If women made any negotiating statements like, 'My experience is a solid match for this job and I am looking for $75K,' they at least stand a chance of moving the needle. The problem seems to be that they are grateful for the job. They are excited to be 'picked.' They don't want to sour the future working environment by being seen as pushy or 'ungrateful' for the amount they are being paid. *That's* the dynamic women need to get over. And for you in particular, we need to get you to boldly state your value."

"What about the whole 'not until Q1' thing?"

Liz raised a hand dismissively. "That's just a way to put you off. In most companies the budgets of the salaries, raises, and financial forecasts are decided back in Q4. They just don't implement them until the first of the year. You can discuss them any time, and this is your time, you are rolling off the success of your first project and they are lining up the next one for you. They know you will knock it out of the park. They need to pay you for that."

"So how do I get my boss to meet with me?"

"You don't," Liz winked at her. "You channel up." Her masseuse had appeared to whisk her back into a tension relieving session. She smiled and held up a finger to let her know that she would be with her in a moment.

"Tell Ken that you really feel the raise conversation is warranted considering your recent success and the future projects you will take on for the company. Then, say you understand if he doesn't have the authority to have the discussion and if that's the case, you would be happy to set an appointment with his boss. Don't let him wiggle out of it. He can either talk to you or you will talk to his boss; his choice." Liz stood up and stretched, anticipating her massage. "Stick to your guns, Jessica. Fight for yourself."

She headed toward her waiting masseuse. "Liz?" Jessica called after her. Liz turned. "I signed up to volunteer at the literacy center." Jessica was grinning. Liz smiled too. It was all coming together now. She felt suddenly warm and relaxed, as if the massage had already rubbed away her worries.

Note From Robbie:

It's okay to channel up to solve a problem. To go to the next person in the pecking order. It may not solve it and it may make it worse, but that's the risk you take. A lot of women are afraid to do that. You have to make that assessment.

If you have to channel up, you should never go behind someone's back in the process. You have to be upfront and forward, or it is viewed as insubordination. You have to tell your boss that you are going over their head. You can ask them to set the meeting or invite them to be in the room for the meeting. It doesn't matter if they show up or not, it is showing the respect to discuss the meeting in advance with your boss before going up the next level.

The important thing to understand is that you have other paths than the one that's right in front of you. It may be with your peers, or it may be one level up, but you need to be able to say – this is an untenable situation. And here's why. If you can do it without emotion or dramatics, even better.

In a good company, every door is always open. You need to use it wisely, and prudently, but every door needs to be open for a good company to function for the long term.

Chapter 32

Salary

Jessica felt the flutter of butterflies in her stomach as she approached the conference room. She had forced this meeting, and as a compromise to her polite insistence, Ken had arranged a meeting to include her, Ken, and Ken's boss, Armand. She knew Armand by sight but hadn't said more than 'hello' in the halls. She wondered what conversations they had had about her prior to the meeting.

They were seated at the conference room table when she entered, making her feel like she had been called for some formal dressing down rather than a meeting that she had pushed for. After a beat, Armand stood up and shook her hand, Ken remained seated, looking impassively at the proceedings. Jessica took a chair across from the two men.

With a start, Jessica realized that this was almost always "her seat" at the table, whether there were three people in the room or twenty. She had called this seat as "her place" that first time she screwed up her courage to sit at the table, and she had been clinging to it ever since. She only noticed now because the rest of the room was empty and would remain so.

Across the table, Armand and Ken looked at her expectantly. She had called the meeting and they were going to let her take the lead for the moment. Jessica cleared her throat and pulled a few papers from the folder she had placed on the table.

"Thank you for taking the time to meet with me," she glanced at Armand, and he was looking at her with some curiosity. Ken was still looking at her flatly, his displeasure apparent. She decided to focus her attention on Armand instead. "I have here the latest reports on the launch of the new product line. For all intents and purposes, it's been a successful addition to the company." She slid the two stapled reports across the table to each man and pulled out two more bundles.

"These," she gestured to the papers in front of her, "are the complimentary emails I've received for my work. They are from vendors, sales people, and even you Ken," she tried to smile to add warmth and possibly gratitude to her voice. Ken glanced at the second bundle as she passed them over, probably wondering when he had ever said something complimentary to her in writing.

"I realize that the company has designated times

to discuss raises, but I think one of those times should be in the pause between one successful project ending and another one beginning." This was the moment that Liz had coached her for. Against all of her instincts, Jessica shut her mouth and let the silence drag out.

Armand studied the two reports she had brought to the table. He seemed fixated on the numbers her product line had produced so far. Ken flipped through the complimentary email pile, seeming just scanning for the names of her fans or to find his own comments among the group.

After a painful silence, where Jessica tried her hardest not to squirm, Armand finally cleared his throat. "You've done good work," he closed the reports and tapped them on the table to straighten the pages. "But Ken is right, it is unusual to discuss raises at this time of year."

Jessica met his eyes and smiled, refusing to back down, refusing to speak out and ruin her chances. She let her eyes say everything for her. *I have earned this.*

He held her gaze for a moment and cleared his throat again, making it seem like he had just been pausing for effect rather than closing the door altogether. "So I would like this conversation to remain confidential."

Jessica tried to smother the triumph that was blooming in her chest. She was going to win.

"I understand," she said carefully.

"The product line that you launched isn't going to generate a lot of income in the short run."

"Correct," she allowed. "It was always intended to keep the company from losing clients. It is the linchpin that bridges the legacy product line from the 2.0 products coming down the pipeline. While the product line I just launched was a stopgap for client loss, the 2.0 products will attract new clients to us." *I know the value of what I created and what you want me to do next.*

Liz had advised Jessica to be prepared to talk numbers in case they asked her to put a number to her value. The folder contained another sheet with the backup numbers for her salary request – however it did not seem like anyone was going to ask.

Armand cleared his throat, "We think you are being fairly compensated for the job we hired you to do. Now, we agree you have grown some in the project you just completed. You volunteered for that project and you did not ask for a raise for that increased responsibility. But, now that project is complete and we spent 1.5M dollars to complete it. As I have said, the revenue to be generated in the short term is minimal."

Jessica didn't like where this was going but she had come too far to back down. She decided to ignore what Armand was saying and hand them the salary numbers she had worked out. As she slid them across the table, she said, "I have done some research on roles like mine and I am 30% below market average. I would like a 30% increase and a

10% bonus for a job done on time and within budget and resulting in very happy customers. Admittedly, it is hard to a price tag on happy customers, but delivering on time and in budget is quantifiable."

"Don't make me do the math," Armand said with a touch of impatience. "What are the actual numbers you are demanding from us?"

Once again Jessica paused and took a very deep breath. She was *not* being demanding, she had been asking. Why were they being so needlessly frustrating? She had *earned* this. Jessica slid the final sheet with the numbers and proposed dates to take effect across the table.

Armand studied the sheet for a second, "Can you give Ken and I a minute?"

"Sure."

Jessica got up and left the room. There wasn't anywhere handy to sit, so she lingered casually in the hall. She could not believe they were making this so complicated. Standing in the hall like this, a few months ago she would have thought she was about to be fired. She took a moment to marvel that she was asking for a raise, and standing her ground, advocating for herself. She was totally calm, totally sure of her value. She could not wait to share this all with Liz.

After what seemed like a long time, Ken summoned her back into the room. When she entered a new piece of paper sat on the table in front of where she had been sitting. Jessica sat, unsure if she should start reading right away. She looked to Armand.

"Please review the documents in front of you. The top half contains a list of areas that we think need improvement and the bottom half is the amount of raise we are prepared to offer you. We do agree you did a great job on the project, but there were certainly many hiccups along the way. Additionally, your *team* did most of the work while you mostly provided monitoring skills. You will note we did not penalize you for some indiscretions at the conference where you were not able to handle yourself with alcohol and both you and the company were embarrassed by this incident.

We suggest you work with HR to sign up for some remedial and social training. They will also process your paperwork for your raise."

Jessica was speechless. They were offering her a 7% raise. A cost of living raise of 3.5% and another 3.5% for good performance. Plus, this list of improvements that was both insulting and ridiculous.

Jessica tried to keep the anger and injury out of her voice. "This is not what I asked for."

"Yes," Ken smiled. "It's what you've earned. The level of compensation you asked for doesn't match responsibility and experience from this one project. You may feel like you are queen of the mountain, but that is not how we see it. Additionally, this increase will not go into effect until the normal annual salary adjustment date. We do not do any raises out of cycle, but it is nice to have you already taken care of. It is a very stressful time for management so one less to deal with at that time is appreciated."

Armand nodded in agreement as he stood. "It was a pleasure to meet you Jessica, but I have another meeting to attend. Have a great day and congratulations on your increase."

Armand walked out. Jessica stood stunned as his back disappeared through the door. She felt furious and near tears. Ken came around the table to leave. He was smiling.

"I told you how things work, but I guess you didn't believe me. I think this went quite well, but I never want to be pushed by you to have another meeting like this with Armand. Please remember, keep this conversation confidential. I don't want any more little Jessica's running to me looking for a raise out of cycle."

Jessica wasn't quite sure what would happen when she used her voice. Her fury and embarrassment had frozen her diaphragm. She might cry, she might scream. She forced herself to take a breath. She needed this job for the paycheck. Quitting today would be short sighted.

"I think I need to look for another opportunity."

"Do what you need to do, but I don't think you can find anything any better than what you have right here. You need to get more experience under your belt and learn how the game is played."

Jessica walked out of the room with her held high. She grabbed her purse and got in her car. Down the block she texted Liz an SOS and sat back to cry out all the pent up frustration. She hated crying, but sometime it was the best release.

When Liz called a few minutes later, Jessica had some modicum of control over herself, but the tears were still leaking down her cheek. Her voice was steady enough though, and she explained the situation to Liz.

"Well, I think it's what be both expected but we had hoped that they both had another side we had not seen. You were very professional but it did not go as planned. It's time to move on...

Jessica took a cleansing breath, trying to release some of her frustration. "I feel like I blew it."

"No, it actually sounds like you did admirably. The problem is that you were at such a low salary, that it would be almost impossible to get you up to the wage you deserve. They already know they can buy your time and efforts cheap. So, you can take all the knowledge and skills you learned in the last year, and negotiate a better opportunity somewhere else."

"I thought women can't quit."

"You have nothing left to prove at this job, Jessica. You succeeded. They are the ones who are failing. And, let me tell you something else. It sounds like Ken is a complete product of Armand, you know what I mean?"

Jessica frowned, confused, "No."

"A leader casts a shadow, whether they intend to or not. People try to emulate a leader's behavior. So if your boss is always 10 minutes late, soon enough, you are always 10 minutes late. If your boss treats the mailroom clerk with contempt, soon enough you do too. It sounds like the culture at your company is toxic, and the sooner you can get out of that shadow, the better. You don't want to become a Ken. Or an Armand, for that matter."

"That makes sense. I think Charlene was definitely becoming a little Ken, before he fired her."

"I'm back in town next Monday. Want to meet and strategize the job hunt?"

"Absolutely."

Note From Robbie:

Every leader casts a shadow that affects the people within their sphere. This can be for good or for ill. Managers emulate the leader's behavior and this trickles down into every aspect of the business. The employees will feel respect or contempt and transfer it onto the next person in the line. This often plays out in the feeling a customer gets when they interact with a company. Are the people working behind the counter happy and cheerful? Or slugging away for an unfeeling corporate conglomerate?

There have been a few times in this story when Ken has made negative and derogatory comments about Jessica and the sales team of the company. Can we see now where that attitude has come from? Armand has certainly influenced Ken's behavior. Armand might be influenced by the boss above him. Regardless, it is now clear that the corporate culture is not a good fit for Jessica. She cannot change the system from within, they do not respect her. It is important to note this lack of respect isn't personal. They made it personal in their rebuttal to silence her, but it wasn't personal until she advocated for herself.

What should you take from this? Two things. If you are in a systematic, toxic environment that is too big or you are too far down the ladder to change it from within, it's time to leave. The second thing is, if you are in a position of leadership, you set the tone, you set the agenda, you cast a shadow. Make your shadow a positive influence on those it touches.

Epilogue
Lessons Earned is Born

From her vantage point of the stage, Liz watched an enthusiastic group of women come into the conference room. They had trickled in as singles and pairs for the last 20 minutes. Now the women were pouring in. At first, two distinct groups had developed, separated by about 30 years of experience. When a few brave young women crossed the divide to introduce themselves to their older counterparts, things had really gotten interesting. Liz was thrilled.

It was the first official meeting of **Lessons Earned** and Liz felt transported with excitement. She would be the master of ceremonies for the event, which included an introduction to mentorship, a brief testimonial by Jessica, a keynote presentation by a powerful female CEO, and a networking session at the conclusion...

It had taken some convincing to get Jessica to agree to speak, but once she had, she had embraced the project with a fervor that Liz hadn't expected. She titled her talk as "Upsetting the Table" and was likening her mentorship to that first speech she had watched Liz give. She had sat at the table. Stood on it and held center stage. Ultimately she had knocked it over and created a new situation for herself.

Jessica was glowing, now that Liz thought about it. After her lackluster raise, she had reached out to her contacts and quickly found her value in the market. With a few job offers under her belt, she reached out to the headhunter from the Scottsdale retreat, and ultimately garnered a well-paying position with a company that promoted from within. She had leaped from the bottom of the pay scale for her position to close to the top.

It wasn't just the money that contributed to the glow, Liz acknowledged. Jessica had met a wonderful man through the literacy program. He was a Brazilian immigrant wanting to read in English to his small daughter. Jessica had blushed when she confessed to Liz how taken she was with her assigned literacy partner. Several months later Jessica loved the man, loved the daughter, and was probably the happiest Liz had ever seen her.

While one side of Liz's brain organized, visualized, and anticipated each step of the event, the other side of her brain was enjoying every moment. Marie had flown in for the event, and Liz had been delighted to see her sweep Jessica into a bear hug. Jessica, surprised, had hugged her right back, two fellow foot soldiers in Liz's mad quest to create this program.

Marie was experiencing her own brand of success. Her app company had recently received a buy offer from a larger medical corporation. She was up to her eyeballs in negotiations and lawyers and couldn't be happier. Liz remembered her first successful company sale and was thrilled that Marie was embracing a similar brand of success.

Brad had also flown in for the occasion and was quietly making a place for himself in the back of the room. Aside from the catering staff, he was the only man in the room and had no idea how to process the seemingly endless waves of women. A few had offered to help him set up the table at the back of the room where he would display the supplementary learning materials during the breaks. He had turned down the help and encouraged them to mingle with the other women.

Liz felt her lips pulling into a smile, looking at Brad. It had been hard to move. It had been hard to have a commuter marriage for the last few months. Although Liz would miss her life in Northern California, she knew she would be giving up her apartment soon.

Change is part of life, she mused. It's better to embrace the future than hold onto the past and she has always been happy to do just that. While the move was one she just was not quite ready for at the time, she was very happy with the decision now. She surveyed the room, noting that these women too were trying to embrace a different future, a different narrative for themselves... These were women who had led the charge and an up-and-coming generation getting ready to steer the boat in a new direction. There was an energy in the room, it made the hair on Liz's arm stand up.

These women were going to shape the future boardrooms of America. They were going to demand their seat at the table. They were going to stand on them, hold center stage, and direct where the energy would take their careers, their companies, their communities, and their world.

Liz always loved seeing her ideas and visions become reality and Lessons Earned was no different... While her initial idea of Invisible Brain Trust had been hard to let go, Ann had convinced her that Lessons Earned more broadly represented the people and the mission of the group. The mentoring was so needed, as was the adult literacy program.

But, now she wondered if this approach was watered down. If perhaps a non-profit wouldn't have enough teeth. There was so much talk about how women were not treated fairly and discriminated against, but at the end of the day, the main people who could solve the problem were women themselves. Jessica was certainly a poster child for that theory.

If every woman did just one thing, every day, to help themselves, help others, reach out, reach up, fight back, or dare to disagree - over time it would change one seat at a time but it would change. *There needs to be a call to action*, Liz mused. A daily reminder that this is a long battle to be won. It is not going to happen overnight. *How can we remind women to do something every day?*

A journal.

Liz dove into her purse and snagged her whiteboard and dry erase pen. On it she scribbled: Daily Lessons Action Journal. She underlined Action twice before tucking it away. She needed to be on stage getting this event started – but she might announce it today, right now, as if it were a done deal, just to harness this enthusiasm into a positive action. No time like the present.

She welcomed everyone and gave her prepared remarks. Before she finished, she paused and then went for it. "Lessons Earned will be asking every woman in the world to vow to do JUST one thing EVERY DAY to move the needle forward on woman's rights and place in the world. The Lessons Earned website will be the primary collective of all the actions women take every day, to ensure we each get our seat at the table, one seat at a time. There will be a Lessons Earned journal coming out in the next quarter, where you can write down what your action was, every day. Keep your actions to yourself, share it with friends and colleagues, whatever you choose, but together, with the women around you, these actions will be an avalanche...a force of nature...and a movement that can accomplish great things. Who will take the pledge?"

Everyone raised their hands. There were even some whoops and hollers and applause. Liz felt momentarily choked up. She had built it and they had come. From here, they could do anything together.

Note From Robbie:

"Secrets." We all have them. About how we did something, or how we made something work, or how we keep ourselves strong. I'm going to share with you now, the secret of my success:

I share my secrets.

Over my career I have mentored 40+ young professionals. I held nothing back from them. If I thought my knowledge could help, I shared. Withholding from people willing and able to learn doesn't serve them and holding back certainly doesn't move feminism forward. Feminism, by the way, is believing in equal rights between genders, no matter what someone's angry Facebook post might say to the contrary.

This book is essentially spilling my secrets to the world. And why not? There are plenty of women seeking guidance in their career. There are more than I can possibly help on a one-on-one basis.

As we saw with Jessica, mentorship is a powerful influence in any career... A mentor increases confidence, teaches how to speak up and be heard, instructs how to take control of your career and provides important networking contacts.

That's where Lessons Earned comes in.

Lessons Earned exists outside of these pages. It is a nationwide program that pairs mentors and mentorees. Seek out your local chapter and find a mentor willing to talk to you about your specific issues.

I'd also like to encourage you to volunteer, whether with a literacy program or some other community-based issue. Volunteering helps nourish your community and enriches your personal life. It can rejuvenate you when you feel depleted and let you see a direct difference you are capable of making in the world.

I would encourage you to also keep a journal. Lessons Earned has sponsored a journal that is designed to keep track of your successes, what you've done to support the women's movement, your gratitude, and the tangible things you have contributed to your community. Writing these daily deeds down solidifies your brilliance and affirms your belief in your abilities. Try it for a few days and see.

Finally, I'd like to thank you for coming along on this journey with me. Writing this book was a labor of love. It's my love letter to all the Jessicas I have mentored over the years and the Jessicas I would like to help in the future. It is my fervent plea to the women of my generation to pass their wealth of knowledge on before departing the workplace.

It is my desire to see a woman executive not just as an exception, but as a normal occurrence. I hope you, the reader of this book, become one of these very normal, very appreciated executives of your field. And when you do, share the secrets of your success, loudly and proudly, to anyone willing to learn.

About the Author

Robbie Hardy has helped countless women tackle challenges in their careers. She spent 20+ successful years in the corporate world before finding her true calling as an entrepreneur. She has sat on all sides of the desk – as CEO, strategic consultant, board member, investor, and mentor.

Living her motto, "There has to be a better way," Hardy is also the founder of Lessons Earned, a national women's mentorship organization, which pairs successful executives with up and coming talent.

CPSIA information can be obtained
at www.ICGtesting.com
Printed in the USA
FFOW01n0540160516
24008FF